D1477152

PORTRAITS
OF 'WESTERN'
4-6-0s

Last survivor of the Star *class,* No 4056 Princess Margaret

PORTRAITS OF 'WESTERN' 4-6-0s

SAINTS · STARS · CASTLES · KINGS
HALLS · GRANGES · MANORS · COUNTIES

Photographs from the Kenneth H. Leech collection

Bryan Holden
&
Kenneth H. Leech
BSc, CEng, FICE, FIMech E

With additional research & drawings by Richard S. Potts

MOORLAND PUBLISHING COMPANY LIMITED
in association with Barbryn Press Limited

British Library Cataloguing
in Publication Data

Holden, Bryan
    Portraits of 4-6-0s.
    1. Locomotives — Great Britain
    — History — Pictorial works
    I. Title   II. Leach, Kenneth
    625.2'61'0941   TJ605

    ISBN 0 86190 075 8

Printed in Great Britain by
Dotesios (Printers) Ltd,
Bradford on Avon, Wilts for
Moorland Publishing Co Ltd,
9-11 Station Street, Ashbourne,
Derbyshire, DE6 1DE England.
Telephone: (0335) 44486

Contents

Acknowledgements

The authors wish to thank Mr R.S. Potts for his assistance with photographic selection, in researching engine modifications and providing footplate comments.
Thanks also to Mr Geoffrey Weaver for design and artwork direction and to Mr Harold Parsons for assisting in the final preparation of the manuscript.

Introduction

This volume is the third in a 'Portrait' series which began with *King*s in 1979 and was followed by *Castle*s in 1981.

Both are acknowledged best sellers of their genre, several times reprinted, and having the distinction of being Railway Book Club selections.

Portraits of Kings took three years to find a publisher, receiving the criticism that the sixty pictures included all *looked the same* — the detail of modifications clearly not being appreciated by those rejecting the book. How different today when this new volume includes photographs and diagrammatic drawings of locomotives which show modifications at the *request* of the publisher!

This selection covers all eight classes of Great Western 4-6-0, presented as a family through fifty years, right from Churchward *Saint*s to Hawksworth *Counties*. It includes pictures of each class, interspersed with commentary by Richard (Dick) Potts, who is again to be thanked for his artistic and practical application.

Full credit must, however, go to the remarkable Kenneth Leech, now in his 91st year and still enormously enthusiastic concerning all matters related to steam locomotives and railways.

Kenneth's contribution to the pictorial history of the Great Western Railway cannot be over estimated. His collection of some 20,000 locomotive photographs is unrivalled and widely esteemed. Furthermore, he has a unique first-hand knowledge of the world of the footplate, having fired or driven every *King*, most of the *Castles*, and many more locomotive classes besides. A truly remarkable achievement.

We did not set out to produce three 'Portrait' books. Popular demand has spurred their continuance. But is this now the end of the line? As far as the GWR is concerned, the answer must be, yes. But Kenneth Leech's collection of locomotive photographs is so comprehensive. So . . . perhaps we have come to a junction and not to a terminus. We shall see!

Bryan Holden
Solihull
August 1983

Begrimed but not disgraced!
No 2945 Hillingdon Court,
near the end of her career,
still a force to be reckoned
with.

...OUTH EXPRESS. G.W.R.

A Dynasty of Great Western 4-6-0s
1902-1950

At the turn of the century, British locomotive engineers were much taken up with experimentation, and the 4-4-0 type, for long the standard express locomotive, began to give ground to the 4-4-2, or 'Atlantic', so-called because it had originated in the USA. As events were to show, the 4-4-2 forged the link between the 4-4-0 and the 4-6-0, and the later, 4-6-2 'Pacific'.

After a brief dalliance with the 'Atlantic', the Great Western, under the astute direction of George Jackson Churchward, was quickly into its stride as the UK champion of the 4-6-0. The company's few 'Atlantics' were eventually rebuilt as 4-6-0s, and apart from one ill-starred venture in the shape of a 4-6-2, No 111 *The Great Bear* (later rebuilt as a *Castle*) this arrangement became the standard for all express passenger as well as several classes of mixed traffic and fast freight locomotives for the next fifty years.

The forerunner in this distinctive lineage of Great Western 4-6-0s was No 100 (later No 2900 *William Dean*) which made its appearance in 1902. It was one of Dean's last experimental locomotives, but owed much to the design influence of his Swindon deputy, and eventual successor, G. J. Churchward, who continued his experiments with both 4-4-2 and 4-6-0 arrangements, and for a number of years persevered with both types. No 100 was joined by two further experimental 4-6-0s, No 98 (essentially Churchward's first 4-6-0) and No 171, subsequently rebuilt as an 'Atlantic' for a fairer comparison.

Saints

As events turned out, No 98 (later No 2998 *Ernest Cunard*) proved to be the prototype for the series of two-cylinder 4-6-0 *Saints*, as they became generally known from names carried by Nos 2911-30. No 2901 *Lady Superior* was the first production-built *Saint*, being a two-cylinder single expansion locomotive with Stephenson link valve-gear; it was also the first modern British steam locomotive to be fitted with a superheated boiler.

Between 1910-30, the *Saints* were accepted as being the most popular tender engines on the GWR. Free steaming (Swindon standard No 1 boiler) easy running — although the two cylinders outside made riding a bit rough at times — and extremely powerful, they shared as equals the main line work with the four-cylinder 'Stars'.

Originally built as an experimental two-cylinder 4-6-0 engine, No 171 Albion was subsequently rebuilt by Churchward as a 4-4-2 for comparison purposes.

(Photo: Raphael Tuck & Sons 'Famous Express' series)

De Glehn four-cylinder 4-4-2 French compound locomotive, No 102 La France imported by the GWR for test against No 171 Albion.

9

Stars

In April 1906, just when the two-cylinder 4-6-0 *Saint*s were apparently standardised as the future Great Western main line express engines, Churchward sprang a surprise on locomotive enthusiasts by producing No 40, a four-cylinder 4-4-2. She was a non-compound equivalent to the three French compounds Nos 102-4, which had been imported for test against the two-cylinder No 171 *Albion* (later No 2971); they must have impressed Churchward greatly for him to produce a new design of engine, after the later two 'Frenchmen' had been in service less than a year. So great was No 40's influence on locomotive designs that she became the prototype of all Great Western express engines right to the end of steam as a motive power.

No 40 was named *North Star* after a few months in service — not altogether free from minor troubles — and was rebuilt as a 4-6-0 in 1909, with the running number altered to 4000. Even this was not her last development, for in 1929 she was rebuilt as a *Castle* and was only withdrawn in 1957, with 2,110,396 miles in all to her credit, of which 850,000 were done as a *Star*. She carried her original main frames to the end.

The *Star*s were the four-cylinder and the *Saint*s the two-cylinder variants of the same basic starting point of boiler and wheel dimensions; and between 1907-23 were the mainstay of Great Western express running, until the full introduction of the *Castle*s and later, the *King*s.

No 103 President, *one of three de Glehn four-cylinder 4-4-2 compound engines purchased for comparison tests alongside Churchward-designed locomotives.*

No 40 *as a four-cylinder 4-4-2, the non-compound equivalent of the three French compounds*
No 40 *was named* North Star *after a few months in service and in 1909 was rebuilt as a 4-6-0, and numbered 4000. In 1929 she was rebuilt as a* Castle.

The first true *Star* was No 4001 *Dog Star*, into which Churchward set his arrangement of the Belgian Walschaerts valve-gear between the frames to work with the inside and the outside piston valves. It was controlled by a screw reverser in the cab. The standard No 1 boiler was developed at the same time and although early 4-6-0s had no superheaters, all *Stars* eventually received them; No 4031 *Queen Mary*, and sequent locomotives being fitted with superheaters, as built.

Footplatemen had a very high opinion of *Stars* for their free-steaming and smooth riding; being four cylindered, the engine was more accurately balanced and better suited to high-speed running. However, inside mechanism was difficult to reach for lubrication and adjustment, hence maintenance costs were higher than those of *Saints*. Another design disadvantage on the *Saints* and early *Stars* was the extremely uncomfortable driving position, since the reverser assembly took-up the whole of the driver's side of the cab, although on later engines this was compensated by moving it forward some two feet.

In terms of power capacity there was little to choose between *Saints* and *Stars*, but the latter, notably for their smooth-riding characteristics, were put in charge of the heaviest trains, and even as late as 1950 several survivors stationed at Bath Road, Bristol, were frequently to be seen working the 'Merchant Venturer' express, particularly No 4056 *Princess Margaret*, which some enginemen considered to be the equal of any *Castle*.

Castles

Until 1922, the Great Western *Star* was indisputably the most powerful passenger locomotive in Great Britain, but in that year the Great Northern and North Eastern railways usurped the title with the introduction of the Doncaster-built, Gresley 'Pacifics'. In August 1923, the Great Western answered this challenge when C. B. Collett's new 4-6-0 No 4073 *Caerphilly Castle* was unveiled, at the British Empire Exhibition, Wembley, London. It was the perfect riposte, for with the *Castle*s nominal tractive effort of 31,625lb/in² the publicity-conscious Great Western could again lay claim to possessing 'Britain's most powerful express passenger locomotive'.

On close examination it was seen that Collett had followed the Churchward tradition, insomuch as the *Castle* was little more than a larger-boilered version of the *Star*. Originally Collett had intended using the free-steaming boiler fitted to the 47XX fast freight locomotives, introduced in 1919, but it would have put the axle-load above laid-down limits. So a new boiler was designed along with modifications to the firegrate area; S-shaped outside steam pipes; lengthened frames at the back-end (which accommodated a larger cab with a roof extension and side windows) and the unexpected luxury of tip-up seats for the crew. The *Castle* was a generous 10 per cent more powerful than the *Star* and to provide this greater power the diameter of the cylinders was increased from 15in to 16in.

Churchward two-cylinder 4-4-2, No 172 Quicksilver designed in tandem with No 40, for comparison tests with the de Glehn compounds.

Post-war, many *Castle*s received internal modifications, but the most far-reaching changes took place in 1946 with the introduction of a three-row superheater in place of the two-row previously used throughout. This foreshadowed even greater design changes, and in 1947 F. W. Hawksworth went a stage further when No 5049 *Earl of Plymouth* was the first to be fitted with a new boiler with a four-row superheater. The final development was reached in 1957, when No 4090, *Dorchester Castle* was fitted a double chimney (the second Castle so modified) and a four-row superheater boiler.

Kings

Four years after the appearance of the *Caerphilly Castle*, and almost before the euphoria for the new class had died down, the Great Western was back in the headlines with a new class of locomotive, the ultimate in 4-6-0 design, No 6000 *King George V*. Conjecture still prevails as to the reason for building the *Kings* and perhaps the whole truth of the matter will never be known. It has been suggested that the GWR directorate saw them primarily as a means of putting the Southern Railway's new 4-6-0 *Lord Nelson* class (which boasted a higher nominal tractive effort than the *Castle*s) well and truly in the shade, and thus to win back the much coveted blue-riband. The fact that no further *King*s were built after the original thirty, whereas *Castle*s continued to roll off Swindon's 'A' shop production line right upto 1950, has been seen by some critics as proof-positive of this viewpoint.

Although 4-6-0 evolution continued in the design of the *King*s, there appeared only slight deviations from established principles. Simply speaking, they were an enlarged *Castle*. Sir Felix Pole, the General Manager of the GWR, took a great interest in the design, even down to small details, and it was under pressure from him that the driving wheels were reduced in diameter from the standard 6ft 8½in, and the cylinders, at least on the first engine of the class, increased to the odd dimension of 16¼in diameter, so as to obtain a figure for nominal tractive effort of over 40,000lb.

The unique bogie, with the leading wheels in outside bearings while the trailing wheels had the bearings inside, was due to the late A. W. J. Dymond, then a senior draughtsman at Swindon, who found himself unable otherwise to get adequate side-play on the leading wheels. He put this design suggestion to Hawksworth, then Chief Draughtsman, who had tried and failed to find an alternative arrangement, and subsequently, Collett accepted it. The leading wheels of the bogie and the trailing coupled wheels needed more flexible springing, and the sideplay at first allowed to the trailing coupled wheels to ease the traverse of curves was done away with, leaving a rigid wheelbase of

16ft 3in; this long wheelbase no doubt contributed to the steady riding of the class at speed.

Many of the *King*s best performances were recorded in their closing years of service, when fitted with four-row superheaters and double blast-pipe and chimney. With these final BR modifications, made primarily to maintain performance on poor quality coal, they became virtually 'Super-*King*s'.

Halls

In 1924 locomotive No 2925 *Saint Martin* (later renumbered 4900) was rebuilt with 6ft 0in driving wheels and a large side cab window, becoming the prototype for the *Hall* class. They were the first engines of the 4-6-0 type intended for mixed traffic (the Highland Railway 'Castles' were essentially passenger engines and so were the North Western 'Experiments'), but they were 'imitated' in a big way by the LMS 'Black Fives' and the LNE B1 Class; a tribute to their proven usefulness.

After four years, No 4901 *Adderley Hall* appeared as the first genuine *Hall*, the only difference being that the boiler was raised $4\frac{1}{4}$in in the frames and had outside steam pipes. This design was so universally successful that a further 258 were built upto 1943 with only slight alteration. *Hall*s were extremely versatile, capable of most types of work, passenger and freight.

In 1947, No 4905 *Barton Hall* was fitted with a mechanical lubricator to deliver oil to valves and pistons, this modification being in the nature of a feasibility study. The early *Hall*s had 3,500 gallon tenders, but the Collett 4000 gallon, introduced on the *Castle*s, became the norm until the Hawksworth straight-sided type was introduced.

The first significant example of F. W. Hawksworth's influence on Great Western locomotive design appeared in 1944 in the shape of No 6959. Although officially described as a 'modified' *Hall*, 'modernised' might have been a more apt description. Churchward's two-piece frame was replaced by a through frame with separate cylinder blocks and smokebox saddle with an entirely new plate-framed bogie. This design was continued into the Hawksworth *Counties* which followed some twelve months later. Nos 6959-69 appeared without nameplates and side windows, but these were added after the war.

At first, the 'modified' *Hall*s showed little, if any, advantage over their predecessors, having the same No 1 standard boiler, cylinder and wheel dimensions, but from No 6971 *Athelhampton Hall* onwards many improvements took place, the first of these being the introduction of a three-row super-heated boiler, and from No 7910 *Hown Hall* the fitting of mechanical lubricators.

The final modification was effected in 1956 when 'improved draughting' was introduced with plain blastpipe and a slightly narrower chimney with no capuchon, thus enabling them to steam even better and burn almost anything from poor quality coal to ovoids and brickettes. The higher superheat made *Hall*s faster and stronger, while the through frames made the whole ensemble tighter with less boiler movement and much less vibration from the motion than with the Churchward/Collett *Hall*s.

When in their final form, the Nos 7910-29 series were virtually the Rolls-Royce of mixed traffic locomotive, but the upgrading had come too late in the calender of steam to enable these engines to show their true potential and future performance possibilities.

Standard Star *type four-cylinder 4-6-0 locomotive,* No 4022 King William *(later renamed* Belgian Monarch) *with the down* 'Cornishman'.

Granges

Churchward had proposed the *Grange*s as the mixed traffic 4-6-0 of his range of locomotives on the Great Western Railway as far back as 1901. However, when the time came to build them he was so impressed with a report on work done by American 'Moguls' that in 1911 he put in hand the 2-6-0 43XX class instead of the *Grange*s. A 2-6-0 was obviously cheaper to build than a 4-6-0, and if it would do the work asked of it — and it did! — so much the better.

But by 1936 the earlier 43XXs were almost worn out and loads were becoming heavier, so it was decided to build the *Grange*s, using wheels and valve gear from the 43XX. Everything else was to be the same as the *Hall*s — except the cylinders. Although these were available, it was decided to introduce a new design with the piston valves 2½in further away from the centreline of the cylinder bores. This would enable the 43XX valve gear to be used, whilst bringing the cylinder centrelines on the centreline of the driving wheels, instead of 2½in above the wheel centreline, as on all the early Churchward outside cylinder engines, including the 43XX class.

It was not the higher position of the piston valves in relation to the cylinder centreline which necessitated the section of raised footplate above the cylinder, by which a *Grange* (or a *Manor*) could be at once recognised, but the fact that on the new design of cylinder the steam

No 2930 Saint Vincent. *A Standard* Saint *type locomotive, the outcome of Churchward's experiments with two-cylinder 4-6-0s.*

chest was arranged eccentrically upwards in relation to the valve spindle.

In the *Hall*s the steam chest lower wall was actually a section of the main cylinder barrel, but on the *Grange*s there was, in fact, an air space between the steam chest and the cylinder barrel, a definite improvement in design which may have reduced the cylinder wear in relation to the *Hall*s. It is even likely that the improved steam chest may have contributed to the free-running reputation of the *Grange*s as a class.

Certainly, if a consensus had been taken amongst footplatemen as to which class of 'Western' 4-6-0 they preferred to work on, there is little doubt that the majority would have settled for the *Grange*. Being set slightly lower than the *Hall*s the 68XX rode steadily, but the smaller driving wheels increased footplate vibration, giving enginemen a vibro-massage via the soles of their feet!

Improved draughting modifications to the blastpipe and chimney were the only significant changes from the original design, and this brought about the expected improvement in steaming. At the same time, it heightened the engine's ability to burn poor quality coal and the ovoids of compressed coaldust, which in the latter days were passed-off as locomotive fuel.

Manors

Shortly after the advent of the *Grange*s, a lighter version of the same locomotive was built expressly for working over the more fragile of the GW branch lines, particularly the Cambrian, where many Victorian-built 4-4-0 'Dukes' and Dean Goods were still in regular service.

At first, the *Manor*s, as they were named, were a disappointment and did not match up to the *Grange*s, having neither their steaming ability nor 'guts'. Even so, thirty engines were built between 1938-50 without modification; but, in 1952, No 7818 *Granville Manor* was taken into Swindon Works and subjected to rigorous controlled steaming tests under the skilful direction of the now legendary S.O.Ell. From thence, the *Manor* was transformed into a fast-moving and free-steaming machine, although the only exterior difference was a narrower chimney without capuchon. But there was, however, a distinct change in the sound of the engine due to the new plain blastpipe and the former rather muffled 'cough' of its exhaust beat became more strident and strained.

Counties

There were a number of puzzling things about the *Counties* Nos 1000-29, the last truly Great Western 4-6-0 design to be built at Swindon. Not the least of the puzzles was why these engines were built at all. Moreover, why depart from the well-tried Swindon boiler arrangement of tubes in vertical rows and arrange them in horizontal rows? Perhaps the decision to raise the boiler working pressure to the extra high pressure of $280lb/in^2$ may have had something to do with it, but it is difficult to see why.

However, one matter is beyond doubt, the *Counties* boilers were based on the boilers of the LMS 2-8-0 engines which Swindon had been building during the war, and that the existing flanging plates were used for the *Counties*. In most aspects, the boilers of both classes were very nearly identical.

Unfortunately, the engines showed themselves to be poor steamers and unable to tackle long non-stop runs without losing time due to shortage of steam. No 1000 *County of Middlesex* was fitted with a double chimney, and had her own curious characteristics. When driven reasonably hard, the effect of the blast was so strong as to lift the fire off the firebars; when driven lightly she would not steam.

Evolution played little part in their design, for as introduced on No 6959, the frames went through to the buffer beam with separate cylinder castings, smokebox saddle and the new plate-frame bogie. Non-standard driving wheels, 6ft 3in, were fitted beneath a straight splasher. It is fair to say that there were outlying sections of the main lines where a two-cylinder engine with the same tractive effort as a

Castle, but with smaller wheels and Stephenson link motion valve gear, might be more appropriate than a four-cylinder engine with Walschaerts gear — and a *County* would cost less to build and use a little less oil than a *Castle*.

A niche was found for them on the slower gradients, particularly westwards of Newton Abbot, where their undoubted ponderous strength was most useful. The exhaust beat from the single chimney was by far the loudest and sharpest on the 'Western', and to hear a *County* leave Bodmin Road with a heavy train for Plymouth was an experience never to be forgotten.

In 1954, it was decided to run one of the class on the Test Plant at Swindon, No 1009 *County of Carmarthen* being the engine chosen. After extensive tests, including running trials with a 600 ton train, a new double chimney of smaller dimensions than No 1000s was standardised, which made all the difference to the class, ruining their aesthetic appearance while producing a free-running, free-steaming engine. The boiler pressure was reduced to $250lb/in^2$ at the same time.

New also was the straight-sided Hawksworth tender which was not interchangeable with any other class — yet another false move. Its main drawbacks were the huge doors set into the front coal partition which made access to the coal difficult, particularly soft Welsh coal which required frequent dampening to prevent excessive dust storms. The older Collett tender was near to perfect for soft coal.

The riding of the *Counties* left much to be desired and they were never popular with footplatemen, being very hard and rigid with a fair degree of vibration from the motion. Perhaps the fact they were designed during wartime gave them the flavour of an austerity locomotive, and although officially designated 'fast mixed traffic' the classification covered a multitude of shortcomings, and in the final analysis they were very much regarded as commoners in an upper-class family of Great Western 4-6-0s.

B.H., K.H.L., R.S.P.

Retrospection . . .

Lineside highlights
by Bryan Holden

Looking through Kenneth Leech's treasury of Great Western locomotive photographs takes me back over forty years to when first I became aware of green engines with copper-capped chimneys. For in those impressionable days I lived but fifty yards from Acocks Green railway station, and came to know the hour of the day and night from the passing of trains.

I saw *King*s and *Castle*s, *Saint*s and *Star*s go thundering by, at night the crimson flare from their fires reflected on billowing white steam clouds. The outbreak of war and years of blackout put an end to such spectacle, but often I would lie awake thrilling to the rushing and roaring of an express growing larger and louder and the bed would quiver and the windows rattle as the train passed in a crescendo of incredible sound.

My first recollection of a named engine was a *Saint*, No 2933 *Bibury Court*. She was incredibly filthy, the last vestige of charred paintwork smothered beneath a grime of soot and rust. I saw her many times over the years but never was she any the cleaner; but I came to have great respect for the old workhorse.

Of all the *Saint*s it was the 'Ladies' I liked best of all: *Lady of the Lake*; *Lady of Lyons*; *Lady of Quality*, but it was such as *Ivanhoe*; *Rob Roy* and *Quentin Durward* that triggered my reading of Sir Walter Scott's 'Waverley' novels.

For me, there was always romance in the air when a *Saint* went past!

My favourite *Star* was No 4018 *Knight of the Grand Cross*, except that it took up so much space in my hand-written reference book! Mind you, No 4040 *Queen Boadicea* was one hell of a 'cop' when she charged past one morning with a crowded hospital train, blue-suited servicemen and Red Cross nurses waving.

No other wartime memory can surpass No 5072 *Hurricane* going hell-for-leather through Acocks Green during a day-light air raid. The warning siren had sounded and I was taking shelter, when the sudden appearance of the *Castle*, dazzling green and glinting brass in the noon-day sun, stopped me dead in my tracks. Only when a coalman, who had tied his horse to a lamp-post and himself taken cover beneath his cart, of all places, shouted and pointed upwards, was I aware of a cluster of black dots high in the sky surrounded by puffballs of cotton wool: an aerial dog-fight!

Full steam ahead. No 5051 Earl Bathurst, *Great Western Society Steam Depot, Didcot. July 1981. (Photo: Bryan Holden)*

Roberts Road Bridge, Acocks Green, where the author's interest in railways was nurtured in the early years of the 1940s. The bridge carried the GWR Paddington-Birmingham main line and was a wartime target.
(Photo: Bryan Holden)

Another vivid memory is of No 5081 *Lockheed Hudson*, light engine, freshly cleaned off Stafford Road shed on the middle road at the south end of Wolverhampton (Low Level). She looked a picture, washed by a recent rain shower, glistening in the watery sunlight of early evening: a perfect portrait of express locomotive power.

Many other *Castle*s took my eye, for one reason or another. No 5005 *Manorbier Castle*, because she was a curiosity, having once been partially streamlined, and No 5011 *Tintagel Castle*, for her connection with Arthurian legend.

It was confusing that some *Castle*s should carry names such as *100 A1 Lloyds*; *The Somerset Light Infantry*, and *Viscount Churchill* (little realising this was the rebuild of the *Great Bear*, the GWR's one and only Pacific locomotive) and *Isambard Kingdom Brunel* (could this be the name of a real person and not some fictitious character?). As for the *Earl*s (*Earl of Mount Edgcumbe*, in particular) I felt somehow they should have been in the *Star* class along with the 'Knights'. But soon I began to identify engines by physical characteristics and less by nomenclature, and was quick and eager to gain knowledge in all aspects of railways.

I became interested in locomotive allocations and looked for code letters, white stencilled on engines to indicate their home depots. Local sheds were soon mastered, like SRD (Wolverhampton) and TYS (Tyseley), while PDN (Old Oak Common) was an easy one; but I was very pleased to come across the likes of LA (Laira), SBZ (St Blazey) and PZ (Penzance) from the south western extremity of the Great Western system. News of rarities spread rapidly, for we had an incredibly active bush telegraph, being aided and abetted by the cleaners and young firemen at Tyseley.

As was to be expected of the premier locomotives, the *King*s were always bright and clean, with an air of power and regality which befitted the ruling class.

My first footplate experience was on a *King*, when a portly, fatherly figure of a driver, in faded blue denims and grease-top hat, beckoned me aboard No 6011 *King James I* standing at the south end of Snow Hill's platform 7. Never shall I forget the awesome moment when his fireman dropped the firebox flap and I squinted into the searing white heart of the fire. Heat scorched my face, seeming to suck the very breath from my lungs, and in that moment I was captivated for all time by the world of the footplate.

Truly these thirty engines were 'Kings of the Track', but one in particular stood above all others: No 6000 *King George V*. Star of the Baltimore and Ohio Railroad Centenary celebrations, in 1927, she so captivated the Americans that they were moved to present her with a brass railroad bell and cabside medallions.

The first time I clapped eyes on 'The Bell' it was a Monday morning. Washday! A day when the fire under the boiler roared like a blast furnace and clouds of steam poured from scullery window and doorway. Suddenly a rumbling of wheels, the shrill of an engine's whistle, and I was out of the house in the nick of time to see '6000' race by in majestic splendour. Around six in the evening she went past again on her return to Paddington.

One or another of the ubiquitous *Hall*s was likely to be seen any time. They were maids-of-all-work, and still I can reel off their numbers and names by the dozen. The one outstanding remains No 4983 *Albert Hall*. Now it reclines in Birmingham Railway Museum, safe from elemental ravage and vandalism, but cold and lifeless, awaiting funds to finance its restoration. Records show that 4983's boiler was originally fitted to a *Saint*.

Memories of *Grange*s abound. Squat-looking and long in the body, running plate raised over the cylinders, small wheels fast moving, never have I heard an engineman speak ill of them. No 6800 *Arlington Grange*, which many times I saw working a goods train on the North Warwickshire line, was my doyen.

Just like the old days. No 7029 Clun Castle *in Didcot Station with the 'Western Cavalier' 25 June 1977.* (Photo: Bryan Holden)

Two Halls *at Tyseley.* No 6998 Burton Agnes Hall *pilots* No 5900 Hinderton Hall, *having brought an enthusiast's special train from Didcot. 15 May 1976.* (Photo: Bryan Holden)

After the *Grange*s, the *Manor*s, short and compact, busy-looking with a tall chimney seemingly out of proportion with the small boiler. The majority worked on the Cambrian Coast line, for which purpose they were expressly designed, and on withdrawal it was convenient to send them to Woodham's yard, in Barry, South Wales, for disposal. Unlike the *Grange*s, which soon after withdrawal were cut-up, melted down and pressed into motorcar bodies and razor-blades, several *Manor*s languished in the breaker's yard until the early '70s, and were then saved by preservation societies.

No Hawksworth *County* has survived the acetylene torch. They were a disappointment, in 1947, when first they made their appearance. Stolid-looking engines without style or elegance, they lacked the embellishment of brass beading around the cab and splashers. I recall noting down the first of the class, No 1000 *County of Middlesex*, but never recorded any others.

End of the line – and end of an era. The last UK glimpse of No 4079 Pendennis Castle in public service. Photographed at dusk from a train passing the Birmingham Railway Museum Steam Shed, Tyseley. 29 May 1977. (Photo: Bryan Holden)

I have been privileged to have had close contact with several ex-Great Western 4-6-0s, including *Clun Castle*, and *King George V* and, in May 1977, travelled on the 'The Great Western Envoy' special train from Tyseley to Didcot and back, with No 4079 *Pendennis Castle* hours before she embarked for Australia, from Bristol Docks.

Dick Potts, the driver on the first leg from Saltley to Didcot, was full of praise for the 53-year-old engine: 'She's still a good'un. No problems whatsoever. Steamed perfectly. I'd love to have opened up and let her go. When she gets to Australia, she's going to show them a thing or two!'

'The Famous Five' at Banbury Station, 29 May 1977 with the return working, Didcot-Tyseley, of 'The Great Western Envoy'. (left to right) Driver Brian Harper, Fireman Derek Sharpe, Inspector Cliff Fletcher, Fireman Alan Tregenna and Driver Richard (Dick) Potts. The following day No 4079 Pendennis Castle was taken to Bristol Docks for shipment to Australia. (Photo: Bryan Holden)

Driver Potts and Fireman Alan Tregenna were treated like filmstars, and while the locomotive was taking water at Banbury, a man came up and offered a pound note for a piece of coal. He was given a lump for nothing, but warned not to tell, for it was feared that if everyone in the milling crowd around the engine asked for a piece, the tender would be emptied!

Five months later, with a sound recordist friend, I spent the day chasing *King George V* on the North-West route from Hereford to Shrewsbury. We caught up with '6000' at Ross-y-Medre, a few miles from Chester. There was scarcely time to scramble down the bramble-choked embankment before the *King* was upon us in a cacophony of blood-tingling sound. 'Great stuff!' I cried, when the train had cleared the cutting. 'No go!' yelled my companion from the depths of umbelliferae and fluffy willowherb. His tape recorder had failed!

My most enduring memory of 7029 *Clun Castle* is of the occasion, in April 1977, when she was on 'The Kingmaker' steam special to Warwick. I was recording for television, as well as radio, and let enthusiasm overtake commonsense in saying that the 'pure sound' of the *Castle*'s exhaust beat, as the train departed from Moor Street Station, was spoiled by the ringing of nearby church bells!

No 4079 Pendennis Castle.
From a charcoal drawing by Richard S. Potts.

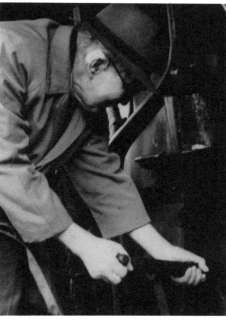

We were shadowed for much of the journey by helicopter, a BBC-TV cameraman filming from the open doorway. When the documentary *For the Love of Steam* was screened, 'The Kingmaker' looked like a toy train, a thin plume of smoke and steam trailing from *Clun's* double chimney as she raced along, her reflection mirrored in nearby canal waters.

But for me the most poignant moment was at the Great Western Society, Didcot, on 12 July 1981, at the press launch of *Portraits of Castles* when Kenneth Leech, then in his 89th year, was invited onto the footplate of No 5051 *Earl Bathurst* (*Drysllwyn Castle*). Soon he was firing with practised ease and precision and talking shop with the driver and fireman. The engine moved slowly and sedately towards the turntable, the other 4-6-0s in the yard shrilling their salutations... and in that fragment of time the seeds of this book were sown.

Ten years after retirement from BR service, No 7029 Clun Castle *prepares to leave Moor Street Station, Birmingham, with the 'Kingmaker' steam special train to Warwick, 3 April 1977.*
The author wrote at the time: '. . . the pure sound of Clun Castle *was spoiled by church bells . . . but I got a splendid recording of the train rumbling across Bordesley Viaduct.'*
(Photo: Bryan Holden)

Kenneth Leech visited the Great Western Society Steam Depot, Didcot, in July 1981, for the press launch of Portraits of Castles. *He is seen boarding No 5051 Earl Bathurst (which he had driven and fired many times when in BR service). Soon Kenneth was in action, and later posed on the footplate for co-author, Bryan Holden, who took the photographs.*

Small Heath 1945

Portraits of Great Western 4-6-0s
Kenneth Leech's footplate experiences

SAINTS

Of the locomotive classes covered by this book, the *Saints*, Nos 2900-98 — with gaps in the numbering — were my favourites. It was seeing No 2945 *Hillingdon Court* start out from Chippenham Station on the 'running-in turn', the 5pm from Swindon to Bristol, which first aroused my enthusiasm for Great Western engines. The locomotive had just had repairs at Swindon Works, but was not repainted. Still, she was smart and clean and it was that long connecting rod with its 30in stroke which specially impressed and thrilled me, absurd though this may seem.

I was watching No 2945 from the up side of the line (where I was later to take hundreds of photographs of Great Western engines of so many classes) and therefore saw her to advantage, majestically moving off into the evening sun.

One evening shortly afterwards, I was seeing my daughter off to Wales and No 2908 *Lady of Quality* ran in on her train. The name fascinated me and I made enquiries of friendly enginemen, discovering that she was a highly-regarded Swindon engine: one driver referred to her as 'the strongest twenty-nine of the lot' and another, Ernie Sims, said with a grin, 'She romped up to eighty-three down Dauntsey just now.'

Eventually, the opportunity came when *Lady of Quality* was working that aforementioned 5pm train from Swindon with a very friendly driver and I asked if I might ride back with him from Bath to Chippenham on the return trip from Bristol. I was duly welcomed onto the footplate at Bath that evening.

When the regulator was opened I was standing in the corner of the cab on the fireman's side and got a mental and physical shock from the terrific impact of the axlebox against its horn guides, due to a serious amount of play that had developed through wear. I had never felt anything like it before, although I had ridden on a wide variety of locomotives in bygone years both in England and in France. However, once No 2908 had got into her stride the knock was hardly noticeable.

'Bert' Jones, the driver — his initial was W, hence the inverted commas for the nickname — was a frail man with only one lung. I was very surprised when, at the first stop, I was invited by him to take over the driving, 'But I'll do the stopping at stations' he added. I later discovered his reason for inviting me to drive. *Lady of Quality* was on

The Driver's View.
No 2934 Butleigh Court
Bath, 13 January 1951.

31

the running-in turn because she had had her piston valves re-ringed, with the result that the reverser was very stiff to operate and the physical exertion was more than Bert was prepared to cope with, if it could be avoided.

I remember that at first it took me two swings on the 'pole', as the reversing lever was called, to get the gear notched-up to the required 22 per cent cut-off. In fact, No 2911 was the first actual *Saint* and the first engine of the class to have the screw reverser. This was entirely in the cab, not partially forward of the driver as on later classes, and caused the driver to lean sideways over the reverser to look out of his cab window — 'the twenty-nine bend' it was called. For this reason, quite a number of drivers preferred the lever reverse, at any rate on express trains where the lever, once 'notched up', normally needed no movement to be made between stops.

No 2908 rode beautifully and one forgot about the slight knock in the axleboxes. At Thingley we attained 65mph by the speedometer with which she was fitted, which seemed to be pretty accurate. At that speed she developed the slight nosing action, self-checked within a few moments, which was characteristic of all Great Western 4-6-0s except the *King*s.

Although I saw *Lady of Quality* often during the succeeding months, I did not have another ride on her, and it was only a few months later that she was transferred from Swindon running shed to the works. Here, the committee deciding her fate heard the chairman, the late Mr K. J. Cook, pronounce his decision 'Let her go'.

So one by one the remaining *Saint*s were withdrawn. Two at least of them were repainted in lined-out black, the old LNWR livery put forward to the British Railways Board by Mr R A Riddles, himself an old LNWR man. The two engines were No 2927 *Saint Patrick* and No 2920 *Saint David*; the latter was the last survivor and lasted until October 1953. It stood outside the Swindon works for about a month while the decision, whether to preserve or scrap, was discussed.

In the end a decision to scrap was taken. It is said that a non-technical clerk at Paddington gave the casting vote, but this may well be only a rumour. There is no doubt that No 2920 needed a lot of work done on her. For one thing her frames were coming apart at the joint between the front bar frame and the main plate frame just behind the smokebox.

A curious point at her last general repair was that the right-hand nameplate and numberplate had back panels painted red, while the left-hand plates had back panels painted black.

Being Churchward's first 4-6-0, most of the *Saint*s put up very high overall mileages, No 2920 being the highest, with 2,080,754 miles credited to her.

No 2938 Corsham Court *on Swindon Works triangle, tender in GW livery, possibly after withdrawal in 1952. Tall chimney, 85C Hereford shed plate. Early version of Collett 3,500-gallon tender.*

No 2908 Lady of Quality. *The name fascinated Kenneth Leech when first he saw the engine, at Chippenham, in the early 1950s. She was the first Saint on which he took over the driving, attaining 65mph at Thingley on that memorable first occasion.*

No 2981 Ivanhoe *in Sonning Cutting with a return St Helen's to Windsor excursion, 8 June 1950. Photograph taken from coach window of the passing 6.30pm from Paddington.*

No 2920 Saint David
(Driver Coles) running-in
ex Swindon Works,
Chippenham, 21 September
1951. BR black livery lined
red, cream and grey.
Note: cut-out in bottom cab
step support, spare lamp on
bracket, red route restriction
disc with 'C' loading classi-
fication.

No 2933 Bibury Court.
Bath, September 1950.
Leamington located, the
engine had not yet received a
shed plate, only a smokebox
numberplate.

No 2906 Lady of Lynn.
Bath, 12 August 1950.

No 2912 Saint Ambrose.
*Chippenham, 10 March
1950*
Note: GW on tender.

No 2945 Hillingdon Court *makes a brisk start from Chippenham. BR black lined livery, Collett 3,500-gallon tender.*

No 2949 Stanford Court *(Driver Bateman) leaving Swindon with an up train to Paddington. Non-standard Churchward tender with larger coal-carrying capacity.*

Time Expired.
No 2981 Ivanhoe, *Swindon
Scrapyard June 1951.*
Built June 1905 as 4-4-2.
Rebuilt 1912 as 4-6-0.
Withdrawn March 1951.
Note: Lever reverser (right)
ATC battery box (left).

38

'The one and only time I came into physical contact with a *Saint* was on 1 June 1951, after only one year's firing experience.

My driver was Tyseley's Bert Tucker, and we were given No 2951 *Tawstock Court* to work the 2.30am Bordesley Junction to Banbury loose-coupled freight, 'H' headcode. It was not a suitable engine for this type of train, but it was that kind of job — whatever was available was pressed into service.

Pulling out of Bordesley Yard, I started to fire using the flap be- tween each shovelful, but Bert said "You won't need that. These engines will steam with the doors wide open!"

On the down grade through Lapworth we were certainly going at quite a trot, so much so that it needed a touch of the vacuum brake to ease up slightly. One could not take risks with an unfitted train. Passing through Leamington, a large lump of coal bounced down from behind the tool-box of the tender scoring a direct hit on my toe. So my isolated trip on a *Saint* remains a painful memory!'

R.S.P.

Saints in limbo. No 2945 Hillingdon Court *and* No 2937 Clevedon Court, *outside Swindon Works, await disposal after being withdrawn from service.*

STARS

As regards locomotive design, the *Stars* were probably the best proportioned engines ever built, the cylinders, piston valves, wheels and boiler all being perfectly matched to each other. They were trouble-free engines until really high mileages had been reached. During their later years frame cracks tended to develop — but as far as I know there has never existed a single class of engine with plate frames on which this was not the case.

The first time I saw one of the *Stars* was as long ago as 1908, when I was able to study No 4016 *Knight of the Golden Fleece* as she waited at the departure platform at Paddington to start off with her train. She was to all intents and purposes brand new, with her polished brasswork glittering in the sun and her paintwork immaculate. I could not help but be impressed by her appearance and the way she set off with her train.

The *Stars* were already a vanishing race when first I began to take a special interest in Great Western engines, so that although I saw a good number of them from time to time, very few were left when I began to have trips on footplates. I rode on only three of them, and of these my first trip was in September 1951, between Swindon and Chippenham, on No 4052 *Princess Beatrice*, when she was being run-in after what proved to be her last general repair. She was being driven gently, and my chief impressions were the beautiful way she rode and the meagre shelter provided by the cab compared with Collett engines.

My next trip was also between Swindon and Chippenham, but was very different. It was on No 4038 *Queen Berengaria* nearly a year after the previous trip, and was on the midnight train from Swindon to Bristol, though No 4038 was a Westbury engine.

The driver told me she had cracked frames, and in fact she was withdrawn only a fortnight later. I had an opportunity of examining her closely at Swindon works, and found that the crack on the left-hand side frame just by the outside cylinder extended vertically from the lower edge of the main frame to about 3 to 4 inches below the top edge. It was a wonder the frame did not break right through when I was on her, because the driver really drove hard and the engine was riding very roughly, lurching violently from side to side.

We reached or exceeded 70mph between Dauntsey and Chippenham and it was impossible to stand upright on the footplate without holding on to something. The booked stop at Dauntsey prevented any speed down Dauntsey Bank.

During the next fortnight I took every opportunity of photographing her on a daylight turn and went to Westbury to get a portrait of her

Leaving Bristol (Temple Meads) with a train for the West of England No 4060 Princess Eugenie, *then a Bristol, Bath Road, engine.*

(not, alas! in immaculate condition) but as a worn-out veteran at the end of a long life with 1,994,759 miles behind her.

My third and last trip was on No 4056 *Princess Margaret*, soon after she had had her last general repair at Swindon, and she was in perfect condition. The date was 13 October 1955, and I rode up from Bath to Chippenham on her. My diary notes on that day, 'No 4056 a very nice engine, quiet footplate, no rattles, and steamed to my firing! A 17 per cent cut-off and a crack of main port gave 66 or more between Thingley and Chippenham. The load was only five bogies, 4056 slipped in Box Tunnel.'

It was when she was in this condition that the top link driver Bill Brown made the classic remark that No 4056 was the best *Castle* they had at Bristol, Bath Road Shed. It shows, I think, how very little margin of performance there was between *Star*s and *Castle*s, even though the latter were just that bit bigger and better all round as regards nominal power output.

No 4038 Queen Berengaria, *Westbury,*
19 April 1952. Driver and
fireman both sport grease-
top hats with British
Railways insignia, but
Driver Hailstone is wearing
'original' GWR-issue
overalls.

Driver Hailstone and his fireman looking at Kenneth's photographs. Westbury, 19 April 1952, where No 4038 Queen Berengaria *was shedded at the time.*

Chippenham; early 1950s. No 4052 Princess Beatrice *running-in after repairs at Swindon.*

No 4038 Queen
Berengaria. *The screw
reverser takes up all the
space in the driver's side
of the cab. It is set high
and well back with the
ATC battery box
jutting out even further.
5 May 1952.*

No 4052 Princess
Beatrice. *The screw
reverser is set lower and
more forward, ATC
battery box set in box
below screw.
26 July 1953.*

*Photographs taken at
Swindon Works after these
locomotives had been
withdrawn and were
awaiting disposal.*

No 4043 Prince Henry, at Bath, August 1951 (Driver Sanger). Note: Small balance weights on coupled wheels.

The fireman is seen blowing out his flare lamp having lighted the headlamps for the passage through Box tunnel. No 4048 Princess Victoria (87E Swansea, Landore) in BR green-lined livery, Bath, early 1950s.

'In 1956, with only three *Stars* still in service, I was fortunate to get a firing trip on No 4056 *Princess Margaret* on a Stephenson Locomotive Society special.

The outward journey from Birmingham (Snow Hill) to Swindon Works was via Stourbridge, Worcester, Hereford, Newport, Severn Tunnel, returning by way of Oxford, Honeybourne and Stratford. A round trip of about 300 miles.

Our load was only six coaches, and steaming was perfect. Except for the long climb from the bottom of the Severn Tunnel to Badminton, and from Stratford to Earlswood, firing could not have been easier. By now my arms were aching and it was as well that I had my regular driver, Bill Timmis.

The front end of the locomotive was in excellent condition, steam tight with the beats crisp and even. But there was a lot of side play at the back which caused trouble when we opened up between Swindon and Didcot, touching 81mph at Steventon.'

R.S.P.

Almost a Castle! *No 4062* Malmesbury Abbey *was one of the last batch of* Stars, *ten of which were rebuilt of* Castles. *Chippenham, early 1950s.*

A fine study of No 4020 Knight Commander, *at Bath, 3 March 1951, with a Cardiff to Portsmouth train (Driver Meek, of Bristol, Bath Road), just five days before the engine was condemned.*

Tall chimney; GWR green livery; large oil pipe cover on smokebox, and elbow-shaped steam pipes, denoting new pattern inside cylinders but older pattern retained outside.

Condemned, but with a full tender of coal, No 4022 *at Swindon Works, February 1952. Originally named* King William, *renamed* Belgian Monarch *in 1927. Nameplate removed in 1940/41 and 'Star Class' painted on centre splasher.*

No 4038 Queen Berengaria *being prepared at Westbury, 19 April 1952. Note: oil cans on buffer beam.* No 5900 Hinderton Hall *in background.*

No 4021 British Monarch *at Chippenham, June 1950. Until 1927 named* King Edward *when name was 'transferred' to* King *Class.*

Left
No 4056 Princess
Margaret, *near
Chippenham, with the
4.15pm train from
Paddington to Bristol,
6 June 1952.*

Right
No 4053 Princess
Alexandra *approaching
Chippenham station. Note:
Lower angle of reversing
lever and the cover down cab
front to house screw
positioned further forward
in cab. This feature
appeared on locomotives
from No 4050 onwards.*

Below
No 4056 Princess
Margaret, *entering Bristol
Temple Meads with an up
express. 26 November 1955.*

CASTLES

I got to know *Castle*s better than any other class, with 757 trips on 149 different engines. My diaries show that I drove on 345 occasions and fired on another 301; and during that time I was able to photograph all 171 of them.

They were always a pleasure to drive, full of vigour, responsive to regulator and cut-off and usually free-steaming. Unless due for repair, they always rode well, being quite free from any sense of 'lumbering along', as were one or two other classes, notably the Hawksworth *Counties*. I enjoyed firing just as much as driving, and even when past my sixty-fifth year a *Castle* was well within my power; although I could not have then sustained a long trip.

Often I am asked for a comparison between the performances of single and double chimney *Castle*s, but the simple answer to that question is that unless an engine was being worked very near its limit it was hardly possible to tell which of the two types one was on. Personally, I much preferred the single chimney type, which made a beautifully proportioned engine, ruined aesthetically when given a double chimney.

On a normal run the only noticeable difference was that the single chimney type with low superheat used more water than the double chimney high superheat engine, and thus once the injectors to keep the boiler level of water were constant, the fireman would not need to bother about that aspect of his duties at all. On the other hand, there is no doubt that the margin of burning inferior coal was improved with the double chimney modification; but I think that a good single chimney *Castle* was better from an engineman's point of view. He could adjust the sight feed oil to cylinders and valves to suit the actual requirements of the engine.

So what advantage was gained in making the modification? For sure, it was not to be found in day to day running, but only at the highest power and speed output; though had the life of these engines been extended there is little doubt that the boilers of the double chimney *Castle*s would have lasted longer than those of the single chimney ones. Unfortunately, the day of the diesel arrived before such conjecture could be confirmed.

The details of my footplate experiences with *Castle*s have already been extensively chronicled in, *Portraits of Castles*, and although I have searched my diaries and racked my brains for any highlight, or even the merest tit-bit, which I may have overlooked, I must confess to having written myself dry on the matter. Likewise, in the earlier *Portraits of Kings*, I have been profligate in telling my tale. How I wish I had kept a few aces up my sleeve with which to win your interest!

No 5062 Earl of Shaftesbury *blasts away from Bristol (Temple Meads). Lamp headcode 'B' denotes stopping train. 12 January 1952.*

'I remember on one occasion, in August 1961, working the 7.10pm from Paddington with No 5043 *Earl of Mount Edgecumbe*. She had a poor reputation, but on this trip she ran extremely well. It was difficult getting the fire bright; a matter of continuous firing — but light and careful — and I managed to keep the pressure around 190-200lb/in^2.

Although the load was twelve coaches, we arrived in Birmingham (Snow Hill) one minute early. She was a very strong engine, as only about half regulator had been used and very little noise from the double chimney — just a purring sound.

The main advantage of the high superheat *Castle*s was that even when pressure was a bit low they could still perform well in contrast to the 'original' version which was very weak if pressure dropped below 225lb/in^2.'

R.S.P.

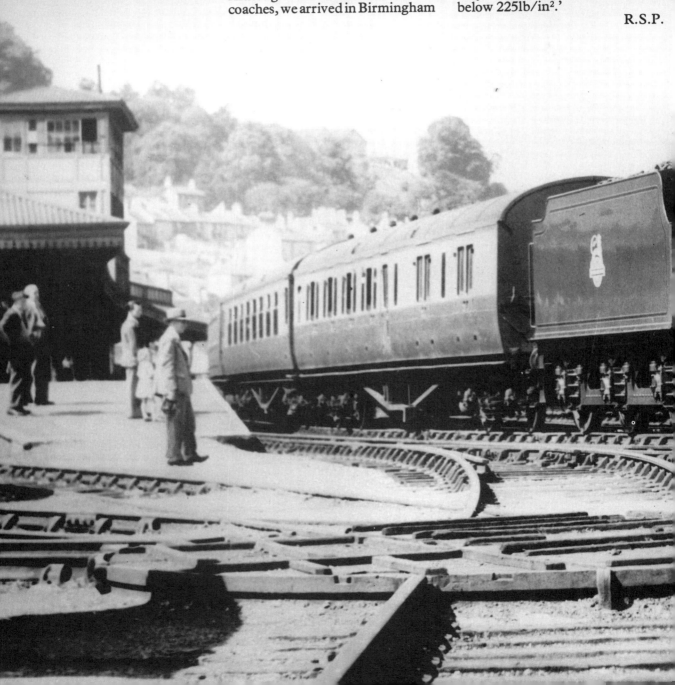

This photograph of No 5007 Rougemont Castle, *Bath, 29 July 1950,* was taken by W. J. Reynolds, a friend of Kenneth Leech's. Kenneth is on the left, at rail level, with camera in his right hand. Many of his photographs were taken from this spot. Except for lining out and smokebox numberplate, engine is in original condition.

No 4087 Cardigan Castle, *Chippenham. Brass beading originally down front edge of cab was removed (about 1947) from all* Castles *up to* No 5012.

'In August 1964, I worked a six coach Saturday evening train from Swindon to Birmingham (Snow Hill) and with Driver Stan Carter suffered the deaththroes of No 7013 *Bristol Castle* (originally No 4082). Luckily with such a small load firing was very light and steaming sufficient, but such was the appalling riding that I spent most of the time standing on the tender!

During the drop down into Leamington, past Fosse Road, it was a miracle that we stayed on the rails, as at about 70mph the engine threw herself about in a frightening manner.

On arriving on Tyseley shed Stan Carter put in a report that saved anyone else from going through a similar shocking experience, and consequently sent *Bristol Castle* to the scrapyard.'

R.S.P.

Another old Castle, No 4090 Dorchester Castle. *Extensively rebuilt with new inside cylinders, new frames, new boiler with double chimney and blastpipe, and extra-long smokebox. Two* Castles *were treated in this way, but only* No 4090 *retained the longer smokebox. Chippenham, 1957.*

An immaculate No 5069 Isambard Kingdom Brunel *running-in after overhaul at Swindon Works. Tall chimney; Hawksworth tender. Chippenham, July 1954.*

No 5041 Tiverton Castle. *A detailed view of the inside cylinder cover showing the top curve with welded step designed to prevent maintenance staff from slipping when working in the smokebox.*
Swindon Works, March 1959.

No 4074 Caldicot Castle. *One of the older* Castles *virtually rebuilt, in 1959, with new boiler, mechanical lubricator, double blastpipe and chimney, and new inside cylinders but retaining 'toggled' frames. Swindon Works (about 1959).*

No 4076 Carmarthen Castle. *Tall chimney; new pattern outside steam pipes; new inside cylinders; new straight frames with 'dished' area around front bogie wheels, replacing original 'toggled' frames. Swindon Shed (about 1956).*

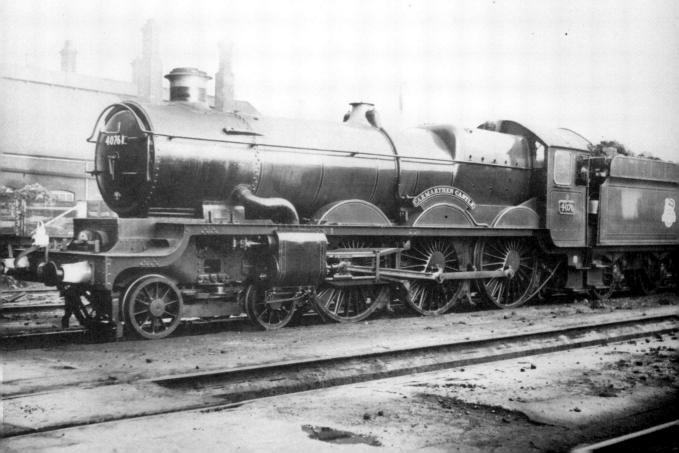

No 5023 Brecon Castle.
Bath, March 1951.

KINGS

It was the sheer power and physical magnificence of the *King*s that really caught my imagination; and I count it fortunate indeed that my first-ever ride on one of these superb machines was on the footplate of No 6000 *King George V* on a running in turn between Swindon and Bristol.

During the latter part of the same week, I was again aboard a *King* and was then invited to pick up the shovel, and so had my first attempt at firing. Luckily, the coal was good and I was able to get it to the front end of the firebox without great difficulty. After all, I had had a good deal of experience on the 10ft-long firebox of *Castle*s, so the extra 1ft 6in of the *King*'s firebox did not bother me very much on a short run.

At the time, I recall that I was very pleased not only at having the opportunity of having a go with the shovel, but in succeeding in firing the biggest and most prestigious engine on the 'Western'. Within a few days my ego was given a further boost when I was again on a *King* and this time had the opportunity of going over to the driver's side and actually handling the regulator of the engine and the brakes.

The fittings on the *King*, being the same as on the *Castle*, came to hand quite familiarly. Also, I was delighted with the powerful and steady feel of the engine under one's feet, and was later to find out that a *King* would run up to 90mph or perhaps more on the level without any signs of distress or quivering through its fabric. Certainly, I was not in anyway overawed or apprehensive in taking up driving or firing these engines, for my experience on *Castle*s had prepared me in great measure and also I was sharing the footplate with some of the world's best enginemen, who were my friends.

During my association with the Great Western I have known well two Chief Locomotive Inspectors — Charlie Pullen (I believe he was christened 'Charlie' not Charles, but he was certainly known as Charlie during the whole of the time I was associated with him). The other was Chief Inspector Bill Andress, and although he was a thoroughly competent man at his job, he was not the rather stern type of man that Pullen was. I always addressed Mr Pullen in those terms and he always called me Mr Leech, whereas with Inspector Andress, it was a question of Bill and Ken. Both of these men carried dignity and authority adequate for their duties and were looked-up to by the enginemen. With Bill Andress on one occasion I had a most glorious trip on a *King* from Paddington to Plymouth and back. We stayed in the hostel at Plymouth and Bill showed me about the town in the morning before we returned on a non-stop express in the afternoon.

As an example of how an engine could vary during one trip according to the quality of the coal, on this particular occasion coming up from

No 6000 King George V
(Driver Dan Norton)
Chippenham, 27 April 1954.

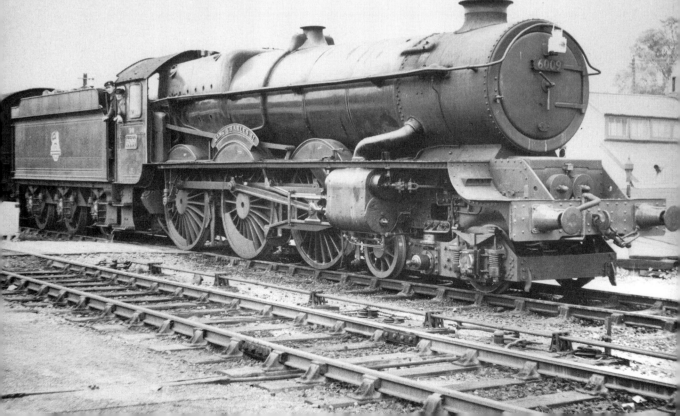

Plymouth we were into a layer of really bad coal and within a minute or two the engine boiler pressure had dropped and the fireman had to get the fire irons out to go through the fire with the pricker to get steam back. As soon as we were through the particular layer of coal the engine resumed perfectly satisfactory and easy steaming.

Bill Andress, as a top-link fireman had had No 4020 *Knight Commander* as his regular engine, and I had purchased the nameplate of this engine when she was withdrawn from service. When Bill retired I made him a present of it, and I must say that he showed his delight and appreciation of the gift. It was always said by enginemen about Andress that he was scrupulously fair and just in his examination of firemen to become drivers. He was not unduly severe; did not put trick questions and was always prepared to give the examinee every opportunity of collecting his wits together to answer the questions.

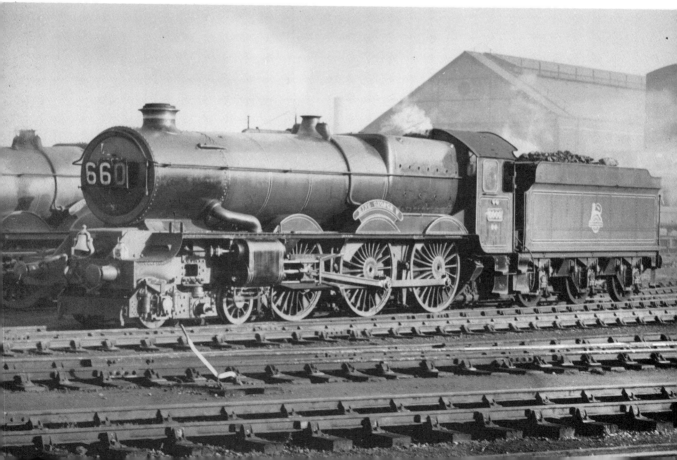

No 6018 King Henry VI.
*Near Chippenham with the
9am Bristol to Paddington
express. 15 March 1952.
BR blue lined livery.*

On the 'Last Trip' No 6018
King Henry VI *in Swindon
Works Yard, 28 April
1963. (Unidentified young
enthusiast on footplate.)*

'My first firing trip with a *King* was on the "Inter-City" 5pm from Birmingham (Snow Hill) to Paddington with Driver Joe Smith. So you can imagine my feelings on seeing No 6000, 'The Bell', coming up the rise into platform 7.

Elation vanished as soon as we got going, for *King George V* had a very bad blow from the superheaters which prevented me from keeping full pressure. The maximum 250lb/in² was reached only when the regulator was shut!

Joe Smith used all the steam I could give him, and consequently we arrived in High Wycombe 8 minutes early, but 3 minutes late into Paddington, because of signal checks.

I had many more trips on *King*s and all went well. Their virtual rebuilding with high superheaters and double blastpipes meant that steam raising troubles were at an end, for they would burn almost anything dumped in the tender.'

R.S.P.

June 1960, No 6025 King Henry III, *at Chippenham running-in after overhaul at Swindon.*

No 6010 King Charles I.
Sleeved chimney. New pattern outside steam pipes; mechanical lubricator in rear position. Cab roof ventilator.
Bath, early 1950s.

A pristine No 6026 King John, *standing in Chippenham. Early 1950s.*

No 6021 King Richard II
(Driver George Green)
waiting to leave Paddington
with the 6.55pm to Bristol.
June 1961.

No 6020 King Henry IV.
Single sleeved chimney.
Swindon Works, 14 March
1954.

'One of the easiest trips I ever had was in 1960, on the 7.10pm from Paddington, with an almost new No 6005 *King George II*. The tender was stacked high with small, hard cobbles, and my driver, Fred Salmon, said "You're going to do a lot of shovelling tonight!"

But things turned out quite different. She was in superb condition and with 10 coaches behind, Fred worked her very lightly, and on about four occasions only was second regulator cracked. For long spells I sat down and enjoyed the passing scene.

Later, I wrote in my diary — "A perfect engine". But from the fireman's point of view although *King*s steamed marvellously, the length of the firebox was a bit too long, especially when shovelling dust and small coal.'

R.S.P.

No 6017 King Edward IV *(Driver Scrivens) running-in ex-Swindon Works, Chippenham, 8 December 1955. First type of double chimney; straight-sided. Brass plate on top step was a BR method of indicating that modifications had been carried out. On No 6017 these were most probably the improved draughting and/or double blastpipe and chimney.*

No 6014 King Henry VII.
*Still retains 'wedge' front to
cab, a relic from its so-called
streamlined days.
Temporarily 'attached' to a
Hawksworth tender, so that
work can be carried out on
cab. Swindon Works,
September 1959.*

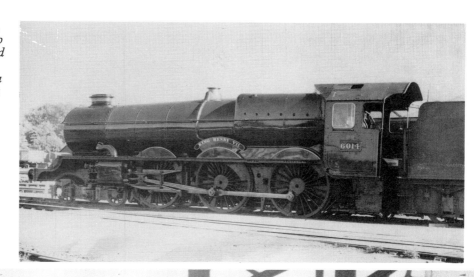

*In the 'triangle' at Swindon
Works,* No 6025 King
Henry III *and* No 6018
King Henry VI *after being
withdrawn from service.*

Three months later
No 6018 *was resurrected to
work a SLS Special from
Birmingham to Swindon and
back – its last revenue
earning journey.*

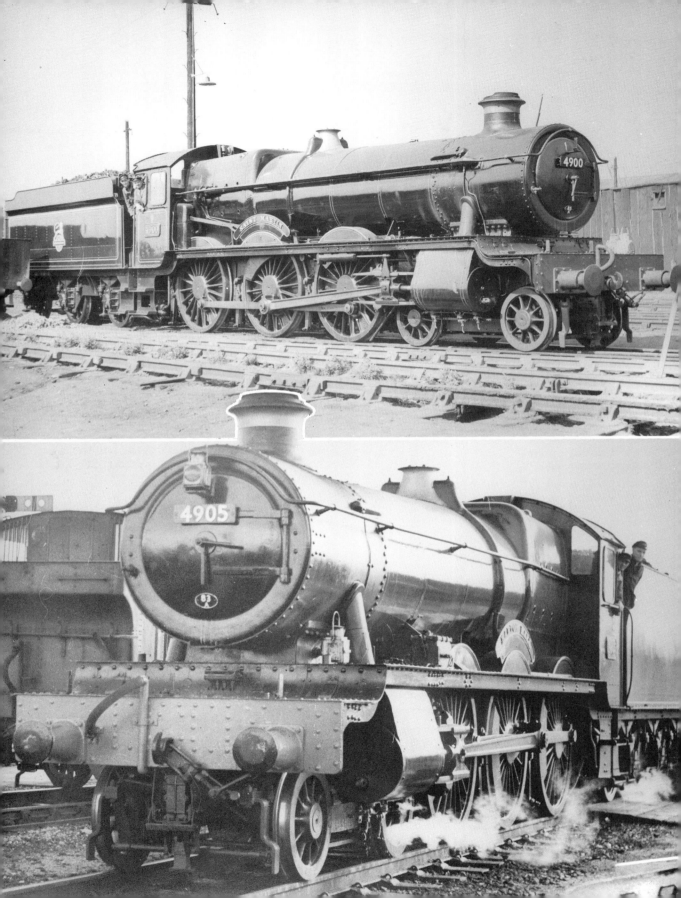

HALLS

On one occasion I boarded No 5900 *Hinderton Hall* at Paddington to find the driver a very worried man. The steam pipe from the boiler to the sight feed lubricator for cylinders and piston valves had just broken and there was no way of lubricating these essential parts until a new pipe was fitted. The driver emptied a can of oil into the water in the tender, in the faint hope that some oil would get through the boiler into the main steam supply to the cylinders, and we were given the 'Right Away'.

I fully expected that we should have a seized-up piston valve at least en route, but the driver drove gently and we got to Swindon without anything happening and without — if I remember rightly — losing any time. We certainly couldn't have avoided a serious failure on a high superheat engine, and even as it was, I think we were very lucky to avoid a failure. Perhaps the fact that No 5900 was in a very run down condition with worn piston valves and rings may have been the deciding factor.

Rebuilt from Saint *Class* No 2925, *in December 1924,* No 4900 Saint Martin *was the prototype for the* Hall *Class. Seen here at Swindon Shed, early 1950s, the locomotive is in BR black, lined red, cream and grey, and with outside steam pipes (fitted as late as 1948) 4,000-gallon tender.*

Undoubtedly, the most interesting ride I ever made on a *Hall* was on the 10.30am from Paddington, the 'Cornish Riviera Limited'. We had started behind No 6012 *King Edward VI*, but it was soon evident that she was not steaming, and though the fireman did all he could and we had to have two 'rolls' with steam off, we took 45 minutes to reach Reading and arrived there with 135lb/in² steam pressure and no water showing in the gauge glass. (Later it was found that the failure was due to nothing more than a spark deflector plate not having been replaced correctly after the boiler had been washed out, with the result that it fouled the blast of the exhaust steam.)

The Reading pilot No 4960 *Pyle Hall* was the only engine available to take the train on, and we left Reading 52 minutes after our start from Paddington. No 4960 was in a badly run-down state and the tender contained a mixture of ovoids and dust which did not help matters.

No 4905 Barton Hall. Fitted, in 1947, with a mechanical lubricator for valves and pistons, the only Hall *so treated until the building of* Nos 7910-29. *ATC pick-up gear is clearly visible beneath front buffer beam. Chippenham 27 July 1957.*

To allow the fireman a chance to get his fire into something like shape, our start was gentle, but nevertheless pressure was down to 170lb/in² after Newbury. Our speed was only 30mph at Savernake, though the boiler pressure was up to 200lb/in². We were doing 70mph at Pewsey, and No 4960 was riding very roughly and so noisily that in the cab it wasn't possible to hear the bell of the ATC system. But by Lavington our speed had risen to 77mph, the highest of the trip, because the ·Locomotive Inspector riding with us thought 4960 was riding too roughly, and refused to go faster. I may say that neither the driver nor I agreed with him, but *he* was in charge and so we obeyed, although at Lamport the driver did sneak the speed up to 75mph, without raising comment!

There were new concrete sleepers in the track near Athelney and my footplate note records the words 'Bloody awful', which for me was excessively strong language, even for the teeth-chattering jarring of the concrete sleepers. The fireman was having a most strenuous and heart-breaking time and finished up at Plymouth absolutely dead-beat; but we had kept the running time allowed from Reading to Newton Abbot, where we stopped to pick up a pilot engine, No 1014 *County of Glamorgan*. I stayed on No 4960! Our best average speed was made between Theale and Taunton, 101.4 miles in 99 min 50 secs, and the load was nine bogie carriages, tare weight 316 tons.

In complete contrast to this trip were two runs from Paddington to Swindon on a late night express which changed crews at Swindon on the middle road. The engines were No 4925 *Eynsham Hall* and No 4939 *Littleton Hall*, and both seemed to me to be perfect from the driver's point of view and as regards smooth riding; but No 4925 was the engine which steamed more freely. Perhaps No 4939 did not have such good coal — but there wasn't much to choose between the two engines. Both did their job easily and comfortably.

The highlight of all *Hall* performances was that of No 7904 *Fountains Hall* when she was requisitioned from a goods train to replace a failed *Castle* on the up 'Bristolian'. Not only did she manage to keep to the running time, but so, I understand, made up a few minutes of the delay incurred in changing engines. Usually, if a *Hall* was the only engine available, a few minutes extra over the standard 'Bristolian' timing were allowed, but No 7904 didn't need them.

Altogether I rode on 187 of the *Hall*s, with a total of 550 trips; 239 of which I drove and 294 I fired; so I think I got to know the class reasonably well.

No 4914 Cranmore Hall. *at Box Station.*

No 4949 Packwood Hall
*outside the weighbridge,
Swindon Works, February
1957.*

No 4921 Eaton Hall.
*BR black, lined red, cream
and grey. 81F Oxford shed
plate. Swindon Shed.*

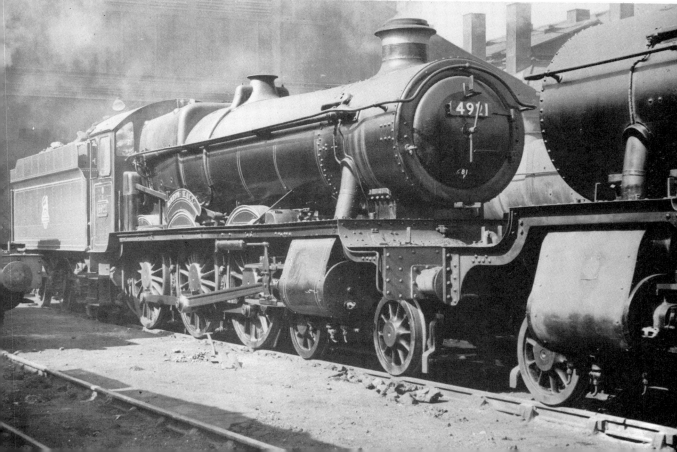

'The most notorious *Hall* I ever came across was No 5936 *Oakley Hall*, which Reading shed used to give us Tyseley men to work the 12.5am "D" freight to Bordesley Junction.

She was an abomination. Twice we failed completely with her, a rarity with a steam engine. And there were times when she could not steam even standing still!

But No 5927 *Guild Hall* was at the other end of the scale, always free for steam and easy running whatever her condition.

One summer Saturday, I had a trip from Bristol to Birmingham on the "original" No 4900 *Saint Martin*, with Driver Charlie Parker.

The whole engine was "loose" and vibrated and thumped, but covered the ground well and steamed very free. When working hard the cylinder blocks were rocking back and fore in rhythm with the big ends.

R.S.P.

No 5900 Hinderton Hall *in BR black lined livery; tall chimney; front number plate missing. (Built March 1931. Withdrawn December 1963. Preserved at the Great Western Society, Didcot).*

At Bath, early 1950s, No 5911 Preston Hall. *Hawksworth tender.*

No 4910 Blaisdon Hall *in BR lined green livery. Swindon Works Yard, February 1957.*

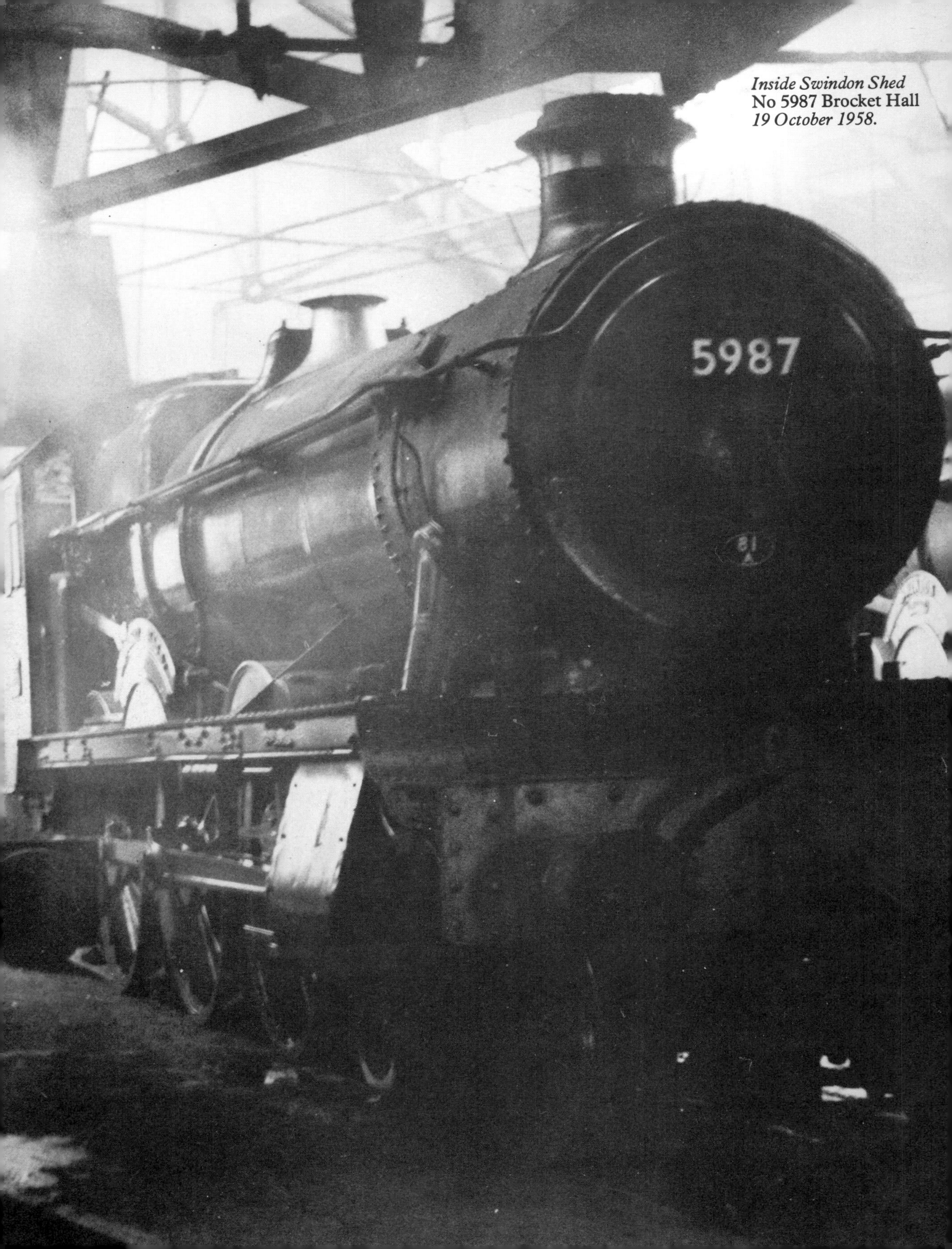

Inside Swindon Shed
No 5987 Brocket Hall
19 October 1958.

No 5963 Wimpole Hall *in BR black lined livery. Tall chimney. Compartment for fire irons between centre and rear splashers fitted to all Halls from No 5921 onwards. Swindon Works Yard, early 1950s.*

No 5999 Wollaton Hall *(83B Taunton) in BR lined green livery. Smaller front cab windows. Swindon Works Yard, November 1957.*

No 5949 Trematon Hall. *Bath, early 1950s. BR black lined livery. Note: AWS conduiting beneath footplate angle edge.*

Left
No 5967 Bickmarsh Hall
(Driver Ernie Sims)
Chippenham.

'On No 4926 *Fairleigh Hall*, we were passing Sandford, near Oxford, at about 70mph when the reverser suddenly flew into full fore gear causing one hell of a noise. Driver Bill Timmis immediately shut the regulator and attempted to wind up the reverser only to find the safety catch handle had broken off, but enough of the stub was left to engage in the teeth of the screw. All the way back to Birmingham, Bill kept his hand on what remained of the catch. He took all the vibration through his arm, suffering a terrific shaking-up in the process.

R.S.P.

An atmospheric day at Swindon Shed. No 5939 Tangley Hall. *Tall chimney. Other engines* No 5974 Wallsworth Hall; No 5020 Trematon Castle; No 5083 Bath Abbey, *7 February 1954.*

Left
Virtually as built, except for
BR *black lined livery and smokebox number and shed plates,* No 6971
Athelhampton Hall,
Bath, early 1950s.

Right
An immaculate No 6956
Mottram Hall *(Driver J Hayward. Fireman Dennis Gwyatt) Bath 21 April 1956.*

When I was a cleaner, No 5907 *Marble Hall* was an engine we cleaned more than any other. She was in plain black livery, so the brasswork really showed up after polishing.

There were six of us in the Gang, and my job was to clean the driver's side of the boiler. My mate, Jim Cullen, had the fireman's side. I always tried to get the copper top of the chimney shining brighter than his safety valve cover. We even polished smokebox door hinges and handles. She certainly looked a beauty!'

R.S.P.

No 6980 Llanrumney Hall
alongside No 73001 BR Standard Class 5. There was no comparison between the two 4-6-0s. The Hall *rode better and steamed freely, and although the BR locos did improve with time, so did the* Halls *with 'improved draughting'. Swindon Works 1950.*

*What a beautiful sight!
No 7909 Heveningham
Hall near Chippenham.
Built in January 1950, the
loco was withdrawn in
November 1965 after only
15 years service.*

Top left
No 7913 Little Wyrley Hall, *Bath. Mechanical lubricator introduced on No 7910 and subsequently fitted to locos up to No 7929.*

Bottom left
Just out of the erecting shop at Swindon Works. No 6983 Otterington Hall *in BR lined green livery and improved draughting. November 1962.*

Below
The last and the best! No 7929 Wyke Hall. *Swindon Works.*

The best Modified *Hall* ever built was considered to be No 7929 *Wyke Hall*, even before the benefits of improved draughting came on the scene. I fired on her many times but nothing exceptional happened, but another Tyseley driver, Howard Jones, told me of a noteworthy trip on 7929 with Driver Stan Sharpe, during the middle 1950s.

They had worked the engine on an excursion from Birmingham (Snow Hill) stopping at several suburban stations to Leamington and Banbury, then right away to Weston-Super-Mare via Didcot, Thingley Junction, Holt Junction, Bathampton, Bristol, and finally Weston, returning late in the evening over the same route.

No 7929 had been overhauled at Swindon a few months previously and was in prime condition. Steaming was completely free, not needing the use of the firehole flap for long spells. Incredibly the round trip of over 350 miles was accomplished on one tender of coal (there was no coal available at Weston) whilst hauling a heavy train of twelve coaches.'

R.S.P.

GRANGES

Altogether I had 77 trips on *Granges*, on some of which I drove part of the way and fired the rest, so that I drove thirty-seven times and fired fifty times, riding altogether on forty-two out of the eighty engines of the class. My experiences ranged from some of the roughest engines I have ever ridden on to some of the sweetest. Altogether, I gained quite a fair knowledge of the class, though none of my trips was of long duration.

My first ride, on No 6832 *Brockton Grange* was impeccable. It was on a down express from Chippenham to Bath, and No 6832 ran freely, without any knocks or rough riding, and steamed well to the regular fireman's firing. I was only a looker-on on this early trip of mine, but it gave me a most favourable impression of the class. Our maximum speed was about 70mph.

Things were very different on one of my later trips, this time from Bath to Chippenham on an up express. I had expected to see a *Castle* or perhaps one of the 'Warships' diesels, but instead the train drew in with an inexpressibly filthy No 6876 *Kingsland Grange* at the head of it, and a woebegone Percy Palmer (not Cyril Palmer, whose photograph appeared in *Portraits of Kings*) at the regulator.

His engine on the down train had failed and he had had to take No 6876 for the return trip; she proved to be a shockingly rough engine, though she steamed all right to my firing. But Percy, who always sat in preference to standing, was most miserable and I guessed he was intending to lose time on the journey as a reprisal for being given such a rundown engine at Bristol!

Whatever the reason, our maximum speed between Bath and Chippenham was only 58mph instead of the usual 65 to 70; and because the seats on Great Western engines were plain hardwood — not padded as on LNER A4s — one's spine felt every jar of a rough-riding engine.

My most exciting trip was on an even rougher engine, No 6859 *Yiewsley Grange*, which had for some time been restricted to goods work, as being unfit for passenger work. Nevertheless, she arrived at Chippenham one evening on a down express (normally a *Castle* working) with a Bristol spare-link driver. He obviously wasn't frightened by a rough engine, for he ran into Chippenham, the first stop from Paddington, several minutes early, having taken only 91 minutes for the 94 miles, start to stop. The load was, I think, not less than ten bogie coaches.

I was invited up, and grabbed the shovel as soon as we got the 'Right Away'. I could see from the way the driver got away that I was going to have a busy time, and it was soon clear from the very rough way the

No 6800 Arlington Grange.
Original chimney; 83G Penzance Shed plate, Swindon Works yard.

No 6856 Stowe Grange *Plain black BR livery. Red backgrounds to name and number plates. Tall chimney; Churchward 3,500-gallon tender. Early 1950s. Chippenham, whilst* No 6856 *was in the station on the Swindon running-in turn*

engine rode that I should do well to heap on to the fire all the coal we should need to the Bath stop, before we entered Box tunnel. This was important, for if the driver continued his style of driving on the 1 in 100 downhill through the tunnel, I doubted whether I should be able to stand up on the footplate to fire. And soon it was clear that he was!

At the entrance to the tunnel the knock on the worn big-ends of the connecting rods reverberated 'bang-a-bang-a-bang' quickly enough, but as we accelerated this changed to a rapid 'bang-bang-bang' much faster than one could articulate it.

I checked the speed after leaving the tunnel and it was, according to my note 85mph — this on a rough engine at 10mph over the speed restriction round the curve at Box. I did a further check on speed a mile further on and we were still doing 84mph; on the level, too!

I am sorry to say that I neither got the driver's name nor the start-to-stop time Chippenham to Bath, for I was too excited! But I have never been 'round the corner' at Box anything like as fast, though I used to take advantage of No 4079 *Pendennis Castle*'s slow reading speedo-meter and pass through the station at 75 on the clock, knowing that it was really 78-79mph.

The only comparable thrill I had at that spot was 70mph on No 5547 on a Saturdays-only, non-stop to Bath shopping train. This engine, with her inadequate pony truck side control, was certainly riding very gaily then.

But never let it be said that *Grange*s weren't free running locomotives.

In BR plain black livery No 6804 Brockington Grange. *Chippenham July 1954.*

No 6813 Eastbury Grange *at Bristol, Bath Road, early 1950s. Tall chimney; plain black BR livery.*

No 6859 Yiewsley Grange, leaving Bath with an up train, in early 1950s. Tall chimney; plain black BR livery with red backgrounds to name and number plate.

At the same time No 5039 Rhuddlan Castle is passing with the 9.5am from Paddington and slipping the last three coaches of its train.

'On one trip, firing on No 6845 *Paviland Grange*, we came down towards Leamington at such a pace that vibration ceased and we seemed to be floating. A most peculiar feeling!

A railway enthusiast on the train timed our speed as 90mph passing Fosse Road signal box, saying to the guard that we were really "having a go!"

We certainly were, and eventually made up 25 minutes of a late departure from Swindon.

This was one of the few occasions I fired to Bob Templar, who did his firing at Old Oak in the days of the "Cheltenham Flyer".

In 1961, with Driver C Parry, I had No 6866 *Morfa Grange* on a Birmingham (Moor Street) to Margate train with nine coaches. I had a relatively easy time, firing with doors open all the way; pressure never dropping below 200lb/in^2 throughout the journey.

The second valve of the regulator was opened only on the uphill stretches, so firing was steady and easy. But there was also a lot of vibration from motion and axle boxes, and the exhaust beats were irregular — in other words she was worn out!

On heavy freight trains *Grange*s just had the edge on the *Hall*s on account of their smaller wheels and ability to move off with comparative ease. Only the 47XX Class 2-8-0s were considered superior. But that's another story!'

R.S.P.

No 6868 Penrhos Grange *is marshalled after being coaled and fire cleaned. Bristol, Bath Road (about 1948-50). Still in GW plain green livery; GWR initials on 3,500-gallon tender.*

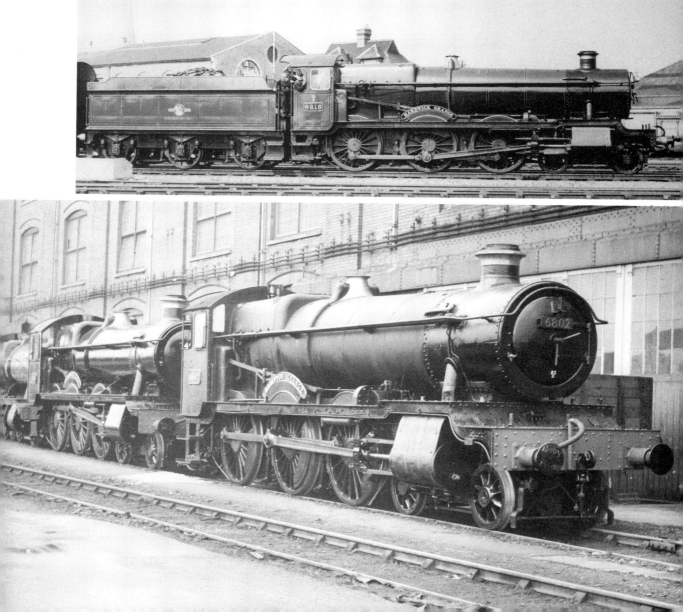

Top
No 6818 Hardwick Grange
on an up local train.
Chippenham, April 1959.

Bottom
No 6802 Bampton Grange
outside the erecting shop at
Swindon after repairs,
together with unidentified
49XX and 38XX
locomotives. 14 February 1954.

Top
No 6856 Stowe Grange
ex-Swindon Works.
Chippenham, 1950s.

Bottom
In Swindon Works yard.
No 6853 Morehampton
Grange. *On a later
overhaul No 6853 was one
of the last engines repainted
at Swindon in full lined BR
livery (about 1964). She
spent all 28 years shedded at
84E Tyseley.*

◀ *Opposite*

Cab study. No 6853
Morehampton Grange.
Typical Western 'pet' pipe
hanging over side. Collett
3,500-gallon tender.

'I cleaned this cab scores of
times when on the "Big
Pilot" at Birmingham
(Snow Hill) in 1950s and
early 1960s.' R.S.P.

No 6845 Paviland Grange.
*Bristol, Bath Road 21 April
1956. Original* Grange *type
chimney.*

No 6840 Hazeley Grange
*approaching Chippenham
with the 7.35am from
Swindon. Regulator has just
been shut and the blower is
only slightly open, causing
smoke (no steam) to drift
from chimney.
July 1954.*

Potts 83

No 7816 Frilsham Manor,
Chippenham,
16 December 1951.

MANORS

I rode on eleven only of the thirty *Manors*, and these trips were on stopping trains, so had no experience with the class on expresses and therefore do not retain a judgement of the class. On my twenty-one trips I drove on eleven and fired, part of the way at least, on thirteen occasions.

My only clear memory of the *Manors* is of the disappointment I felt on my first trip on one, both as regards steaming and power. The engine concerned was in its original condition, but I recall some pleasant, though unadventurous, later trips on No 7808 *Cookham Manor* and No 7829 *Ramsbury Manor*.

They were a class of engine designed and built to come within a definite weight limit, and could not therefore give the feeling of ample power which the other Great Western 4-6-0s always gave.

No 7801 Anthony Manor, *fitted with narrow chimney without capuchon; the only outward change after 'improved draughting' arrangements were applied to increase smokebox efficiency. These modifications subsequently transformed these rather mediocre machines into free-steaming 'fire engines'. Swindon Works, May 1962.*

Fitted with original standard GWR chimney; plain black livery. No 7807 Compton Manor *after release from 'A' Erecting Shop. Swindon Works, 30 January 1955.*

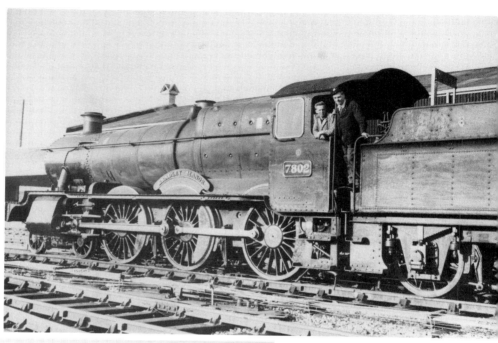

Running-in after a 'sole and heel' at Swindon Works, No 7802 Bradley Manor, Chippenham, early 1950s. Safety bar on front of tender coal space was fitted to warn enginemen of overhead electric wires when working on LM region in Crewe area.

An early recipient of the restored lined green livery, No 7828 Odney Manor. One of the batch built as late as 1950, the engine is fitted with narrow chimney and attached to an intermediate Churchward 3,500-gallon tender with larger coal-carrying capacity. Chippenham 2 August 1956.

'I did not have much experience on these engines, especially in their original condition, only a few trips on freight trains.

After the improved draughting modifications came about I had a driving turn soon after passing at Swindon. My fireman was Tony Weston and we had No 7816 *Frilsham Manor* to work the 5.45pm Birmingham (Moor Street) to Stratford all stations, and return with the "Honeybourne Goods".

The three coach load to Stratford was no problem, but we had seventeen wagons of coke for the long climb to Earlswood, which needed banking assistance from Stratford to Bearley, and this proved quite exciting as the two of us were in a hurry to get home, so we made an excellent climb, making a lot of noise and sparks.

Tony kept the pressure just below blowing-off and the water level in the top of the glass all the way, and I used the second valve of regulator with about 25 per cent average cut-off. A nice little trip.

R.S.P.

No 7814 Fringford Manor, *24 April 1954, Bath.*

Smile, for posterity's sake! Kenneth's camera captures a rather serious-faced twosome aboard No 7829 Ramsbury Manor, *Chippenham, early 1950s.*

No. 7806 Cockington
Manor *alongside* No. 1011
County of Chester *in
Swindon Works Yard, 4
November 1962.*

COUNTIES

I rode on twenty-two of the thirty engines of the class; out of my 143 trips I drove on 56 and fired on 74 occasions; most of these were after the engines had been modified, and I cannot recall a bad trip. My only complaint was that on a stopping train they would not quite keep time if only the first port of the regulator was opened, but would romp away, gaining time, however carefully the regulator was manipulated to give as small as possible main valve opening. They were really strong, lively engines, but their riding seemed to me to be a little harder than the *Castles*.

My most vivid memory is of a trip on a Westbury-to-Swindon stopping train. The engine was No 1012 *County of Denbigh* and the load about seven bogies. No 1012 was steaming well and I had a good hot, deep fire in the firebox by Melksham, when a spirit of mischief entered into me and I said to the driver, 'I'll bet you couldn't get her up to 60 miles an hour at the top of Lacock Bank'.

He didn't reply but there must have been a twinkle in his eye, for my lovely fire mostly flew out of the chimney, and at the top of the bank he drew my attention to the speedometer which was showing well over 60mph; and then I had to rebuild my wreck of a fire, which I had not expected to have to tackle! It was a fair do. Lacock Bank is about two miles long at a rise of 1 in 100, and the summit is about three miles from Melksham station.

The maximum speed I have ever heard of a *County* attaining was 99mph down Dauntsey Bank. I do not know the engine number, but the driver was Bill Brown of Bristol, Bath Road, and the speed was due to a passenger challenging Bill to do 100 down Dauntsey after the Swindon stop. Bill thought he had done it, for his speedometer was reading over the 100, but the passenger, who was timing the speed in the train, told him at Bristol it was only 99. Bill never told me what cut-off he used on this occasion.

No 1000
County of Middlesex.
*approaching Chippenham with
an express, May 1952.*

At Chippenham, November 1955, No 1011 County of Chester *had just been rebuilt with double blastpipe and chimney, and was being run-in from Swindon Works.* Note: Two oil pipe covers on smokebox.

Running-in following overhaul at Swindon – and withdrawn 8 months later! No 1019 County of Merioneth (Driver Whiter) Chippenham, June 1962.

'Certainly the *Counties* were not the most popular engines of Swindon design, for when first built it was almost impossible to maintain 280lb/in^2 with full regulator working.

However, when all were eventually fitted with double-chimneys and the boiler pressure reduced there was a vast improvement in performance. Sheer strength and rapid acceleration, with complete absence of slipping was in their favour. Fitted with single chimney the exhaust was like a short, sharp explosion.

After a very rough trip to Swindon, in the summer of 1956, with No 1019 *County of Merioneth*, Driver Bill Timmis and I were walking along the platform towards the cabin to have a cup of tea before working back, when another *County* came roaring through the station from the Paddington direction doing at least 70-75mph, and blowing off at the safety valves.

We couldn't believe our eyes. "Why couldn't you get ours going like that?" quipped Bill, knowing full well how hard I had struggled to raise steam.'

R.S.P.

No 1000 County of Middlesex *(Driver Tom Wilson) running-in, Chippenham April 1955. Original double-chimney; the only County with this type. Straight-sided tender; introduced with this class, but heavier than those built later and fitted to other classes. BR black, lined red, cream and grey. Built August 1945, nameless until March 1946.*

No 1000 County of
Middlesex *under test at
Swindon Works,
23 September 1953.*

No 1001 County of Bucks
*(Driver Percy Gate) Bath,
January 1961. Standard
cast double chimney, fitted
1957, following tests with
No 1009. All* Counties
*eventually received these
chimneys and at the same
time boiler pressure was
reduced to 250lb/in².*

No 1012 County of Denbigh (*Driver Hector Gale*). *Red disc 'D' route restriction classification on cabside with an 'X' below denoting that loads slightly in excess of 'D' can be taken. Double chimney. Chippenham, January 1961.*

My footplate journeying lasted right upto the end of steam on the Western Region. The *King*s were the first 4-6-0s to go, in 1962, and three years later most of the *Castle*s had been withdrawn, and so I was restricted almost entirely to trips on run-down *Hall*s and *Counties*.

Now I began to ride on diesels, mainly to keep in contact with enginemen friends, and I had plenty of experience in handling these machines, for I rode on all seventy-one of the 'Warships' class, a total of 476 trips, of which ninety-nine were driving trips.

Of the D7000 diesel hydraulics, I rode on forty-eight, had a total 142 trips, of which thirty-eight were driving trips. I rode also on three engines of the D600 class, and the diesel-electrics (twenty-seven trips on twenty-one engines — seven driving) which compared with the 'Westerns' on which I had twenty-six trips on twenty-one engines (seven driving).

I must confess to having treated them with considerable disdain — caning them as hard as I could, hoping they would break down! But they never did on my trips. If they had I would have had no idea what I ought to do.

On one occasion, when I was driving a down express, the WR driver switched-off all his lights and power in the middle of Box Tunnel, just to test my reactions to an emergency situation. I just sat there like a dummy. I detested all diesels — and still do! So that nowadays I never go near a railway station.

After awhile, news of my impending 'retirement' became widespread, and my wife and I received an invitation from the enginemen at Bristol, Bath Road, to visit them. Unfortunately, we had to decline, but my wife was sent a glorious bouquet of flowers, and at a subsequent ASLEF meeting I was officially thanked for the photographs which I had taken of enginemen over the years.

Shortly afterwards, ASLEF Swindon branch made me a presentation, and then I journeyed to a similar reception and presentation at Old Oak Common (Paddington) where I made a rather long speech to a roomful of enginemen and inspectors — so I had to be very discreet!

I must say I was greatly touched by this spontaneous display of appreciation and comradeship: it was entirely unexpected on my part, and is something I shall never forget. Fortunately, this was not the absolute end of the line for me, and for several years more, I was a guest of the Swindon enginemen at their annual reunion dinner.

My years on the 'Western' were some of the most rewarding and enjoyable in my whole life. Never did I set out with any ideas of taking photographs for the sake of posterity, or commercial gain — it was merely for my own pleasure and to give copies to enginemen friends. Neither had I thoughts of writing books on my exploits.

Authorship (except for several technical articles and various pamphlets' for such as the Stephenson Locomotive Society) has come late in my life. It has given me immense satisfaction and great pleasure, not only in re-stirring joyous memories, but in the making of many new and lasting friendships.

K.H.L.

No 1003 County of Wilts. *Single chimney, as fitted to all except* No 1000 *when built. Lined green livery; probably one of the first engines to be repainted green after BR lined black. Bath, 1955.*

Engine modifications and general detail plans

Fortunately, a number of Great Western 4-6-0s have been preserved and restored to working order, and so it is still possible to see certain of these splendid machines and enjoy them 'in the flesh'.

For many enthusiasts, the interest in steam traction lies in a cherished memory of a singular locomotive seen and forever encapsulated in a particular moment of time. The engine may long since have made its one-way journey to the scrapyard, but in skilled hands its likeness can be reincarnated in miniature.

Our previous two 'Portraits' books have aroused considerable interest and drawn favourable comment in pin-pointing salient features, such as different chimney forms, types of tender, the configuration of outside steam pipes and suchlike. We hope that the choice of photographs in this latest volume, and the information given alongside, will be of assistance to those who seek after fine detail.

The drawings of each class show general arrangements and dimensional detail from which scale models can be scratch built. This information has been obtained from the Great Western list of drawings, plans and diagrams, formerly preserved in Clapham Museum, and which are now available as photostatic copies.

Good modelling!

Drawings reproduced by Courtesy of British Rail
© British Rail

Saint (2900) Class
Two-Cylinder 4-6-0 Type

(Introduced 1902)
Designed by G.J. Churchward

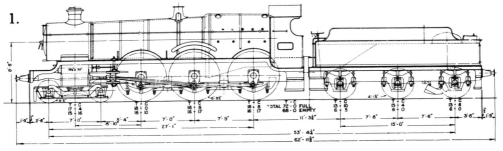

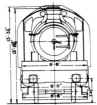

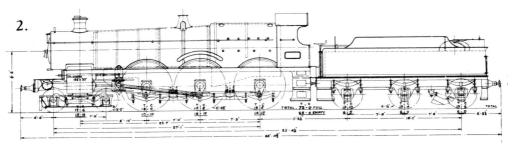

1. 'Standard' Version Nos. 2911-2930

2. Nos. 2901-10 Nos. 2971-90

Cylinders:	Two	Heating Surface:	2,104 sq ft	Tractive Effort:	24,395lb
	Diameter 18½in	Area of Firegrate:	27.07 sq ft	Total Weight of	40 tons 0 cwt Full
	Stroke 30in	Wheels:	Bogie 3ft 2in	Tender:	18 tons 5 cwt Empty
Boiler:	Barrel 14ft 10in		Coupled 6ft 8½in	Total Weight of	72 tons 0 cwt Full
	Diameter 4ft 10¹³⁄₁₆in	Water Capacity of		Engine:	66 tons 0 cwt Empty
	Outside 5ft 6in	Tender:	3,500 gallons		
Firebox:	Length Outside 9ft 0in	Working Pressure:	225lb/in²		

Star (4000) Class
Four-Cylinder 4-6-0 Type

(Introduced 1906)
Designed by G.J. Churchward

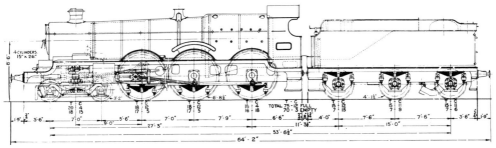

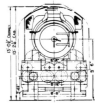

Cylinders:	Four	Heating Surface:	2,104 sq ft	Tractive Effort:	27,800lb
	Diameter 15in	Area of Firegrate:	27.07 sq ft	Total Weight of	46 tons 14 cwt Full
	Stroke 26in	Wheels:	Bogie 3ft 2in	Tender:	22 tons 10 cwt Empty
Boiler:	Barrel 14ft 10in		Coupled 6ft 8½in	Total Weight of	75 tons 12 cwt Full
	Diameter 4ft 10¹³⁄₁₆in	Water Capacity of		Engine:	70 tons 3 cwt Empty
	Outside 5ft 6in	Tender:	4,000 gallons		
Firebox:	Length Outside 9ft 0in	Working Pressure:	225lb/in²		

Castle (4073) Class
Four-Cylinder 4-6-0 Type

(Introduced 1923)
Designed by C.B. Collett

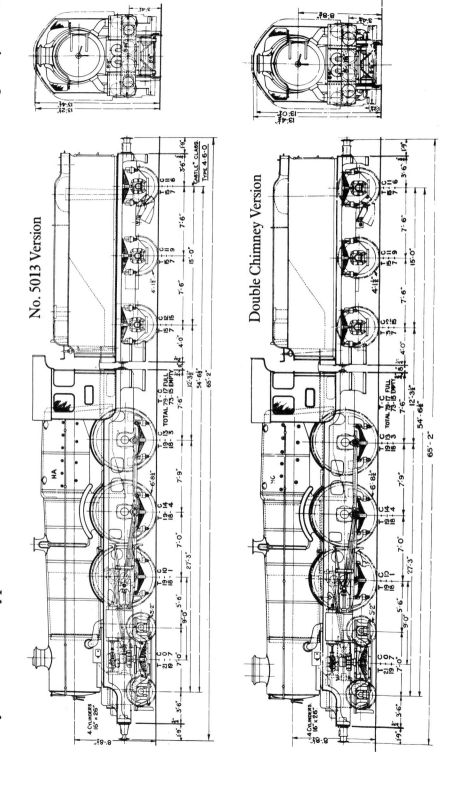

No. 5013 Version

Double Chimney Version

Cylinders:	Four
	Diameter 16in
	Stroke 26in
Boiler:	Barrel 14ft 10in
	Diameter 5ft 1¹⁵/₁₆in
	Outside 5ft 9in
Firebox:	Length Outside 10ft 0in
Heating Surface:	2,312 sq ft
Area of Firegrate:	29.36 sq ft
Wheels:	Bogie 3ft 2in
	Coupled 6ft 8½in
Water Capacity of	
Tender:	4,000 gallons
Working Pressure:	225lb/in²
Tractive Effort:	31,625lb
Total Weight of	
Tender:	46 tons 14 cwt Full
	22 tons 10 cwt Empty
Total Weight of	
Engine:	79 tons 17 cwt Full
	73 tons 15 cwt Empty

King (6000) Class
Four-Cylinder 4-6-0 Type

(Introduced 1927)
Designed by C.B. Collett

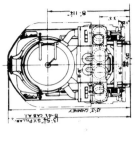

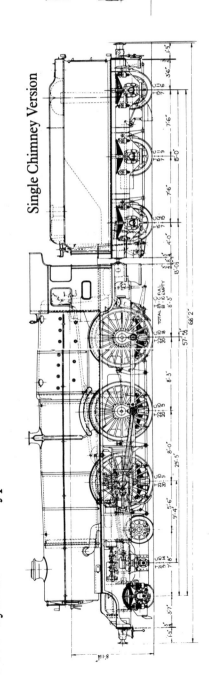

Single Chimney Version

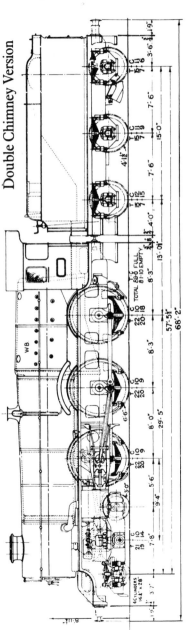

Double Chimney Version

Cylinders:	Four
	Diameter 16¼in
	Stroke 28in
Boiler:	Barrel 16ft 0in
	Diameter 5ft 6¼in
	Outside 6ft 0in
Firebox:	Length Outside 11ft 6in

Heating Surface:	2,490 sq ft
Area of Firegrate:	34.3 sq ft
Wheels:	Bogie 3ft 0in
	Coupled 6ft 6in
Water Capacity of	
Tender:	4,000 gallons
Working Pressure:	250lb/in²

Tractive Effort:	40,300lb
Total Weight of	46 tons 14 cwt Full
Tender:	22 tons 10 cwt Empty
Total Weight of	89 tons 0 cwt Full
Engine:	81 tons 10 cwt Empty

Hall (4900) Class
Two-Cylinder 4-6-0 Type

(Introduced 1924 (No 4900) the rest 1928)
Designed by C.B. Collett

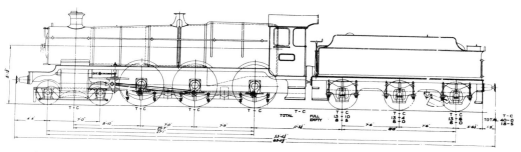

No. 2925 (No. 4900)

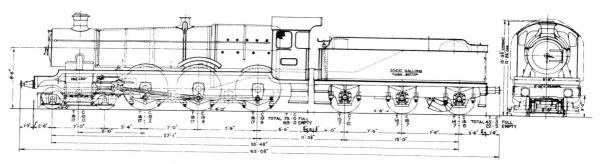

Standard Version Nos. 4901-6958

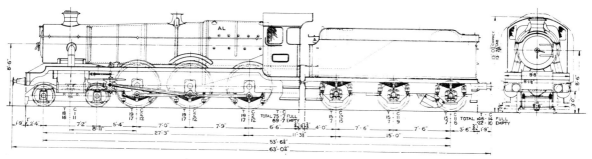

'Modified' Nos. 6959-7929

Cylinders:	Two Diameter 18½in Stroke 30in	Water Capacity of Tender:	4,000 gallons
Boiler:	Barrel 14ft 10in Diameter 4ft 10¹³⁄₁₆in Outside 5ft 6in	Working Pressure: Tractive Effort: Total Weight of Tender:	225lb/in² 27,275lb 46 tons 14 cwt Full 22 tons 10 cwt Empty
Firebox: Heating Surface: Area of Firegrate: Wheels:	Length Outside 9ft 0in 2,104 sq ft 27.07 sq ft Bogie 3ft 0in Coupled 6ft 0in	Total Weight of Engine:	75 tons 0 cwt Full 69 tons 0 cwt Empty

Grange (6800) Class
Two-Cylinder 4-6-0 Type

(Introduced 1936)
Designed by C.B. Collett

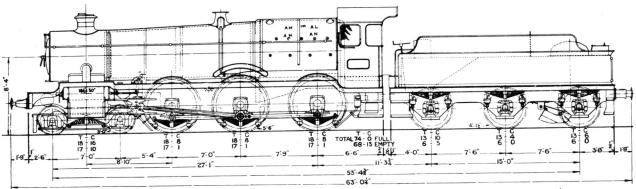

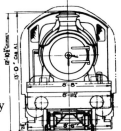

Cylinders:	Two	Water Capacity of	
	Diameter 18½in	Tender:	3,500 gallons
	Stroke 30in	Working Pressure:	225lb/in²
Boiler:	Barrel 14ft 10in	Tractive Effort:	28,875lb
	Diameter 4ft 10³⁄₁₆in	Total Weight of	40 tons 0 cwt Full
	Outside 5ft 6in	Tender:	18 tons 5 cwt Empty
Firebox:	Length Outside 9ft 0in	Total Weight of	74 tons 0 cwt Full
Heating Surface:	2,104 sq ft	Engine:	68 tons 13 cwt Empty
Area of Firegrate:	27.07 sq ft		
Wheels:	Bogie 3ft 0in		
	Coupled 5ft 8in		

Manor (7800) Class
Two-Cylinder 4-6-0 Type

(Introduced 1938)
Designed by C.B. Collett

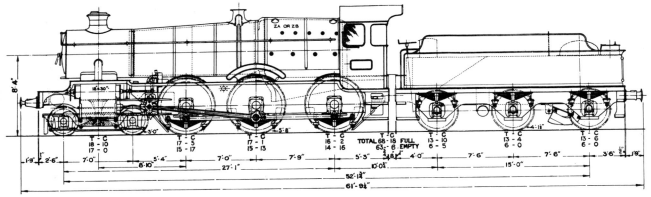

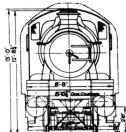

Cylinders:	Two	Water Capacity of	
	Diameter 18in	Tender:	3,500 gallons
	Stroke 30in	Working Pressure:	225lb/in²
Boiler:	Barrel 12ft 6in	Tractive Effort:	27,340lb
	Diameter 4ft 7⅝in	Total Weight of	40 tons 0 cwt Full
	Outside 5ft 3in	Tender:	18 tons 5 cwt Empty
Firebox:	Length Outside 8ft 8⅛in	Total Weight of	68 tons 18 cwt Full
Heating Surface:	1,585.5sq ft	Engine:	63 tons 6 cwt Empty
Area of Firegrate:	22.1 sq ft		
Wheels:	Bogie 3ft 0in		
	Coupled 5ft 8in		

County (1000) Class
Two-Cylinder 4-6-0 Type

(Introduced 1945)
Designed by F. W. Hawksworth

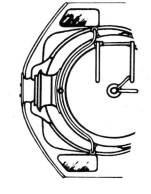

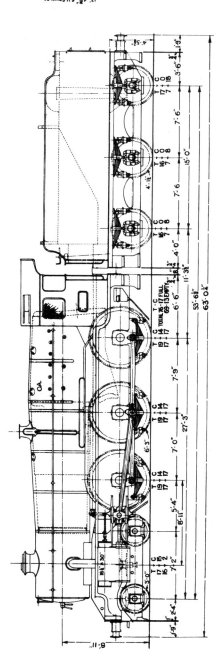

Standard version No 1000

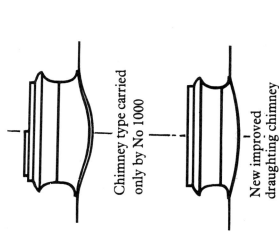

Chimney type carried only by No 1000

New improved draughting chimney

Front view.
New improved draughting chimney.

Cylinders:	Two
	Diameter 18½in
	Stroke 30in
Boiler:	Barrel 12ft 7³⁄₁₆in
	Diameter 5ft 0in
	Outside 5ft 8⅜in
	Length Outside 9ft 9in
Firebox:	
Heating Surface:	1,968 sq ft
Area of Firegrate:	28.84 sq ft
Wheels:	Bogie 3ft 0in
	Coupled 6ft 3in
Water Capacity of	
Tender:	4,000 gallons
Working Pressure:	280lb/in²
Tractive Effort:	32,580lb
Total Weight of	49 tons 0 cwt Full
Tender:	22 tons 14 cwt Empty
Total Weight of	76 tons 17 cwt Full
Engine:	69 tons 13 cwt Empty

Ready for the fray.

Design & Artwork Production, Barbryn Press Limited, Birmingham.